Cooking
IN THE PHOTOGRAPHER'S HOUSE

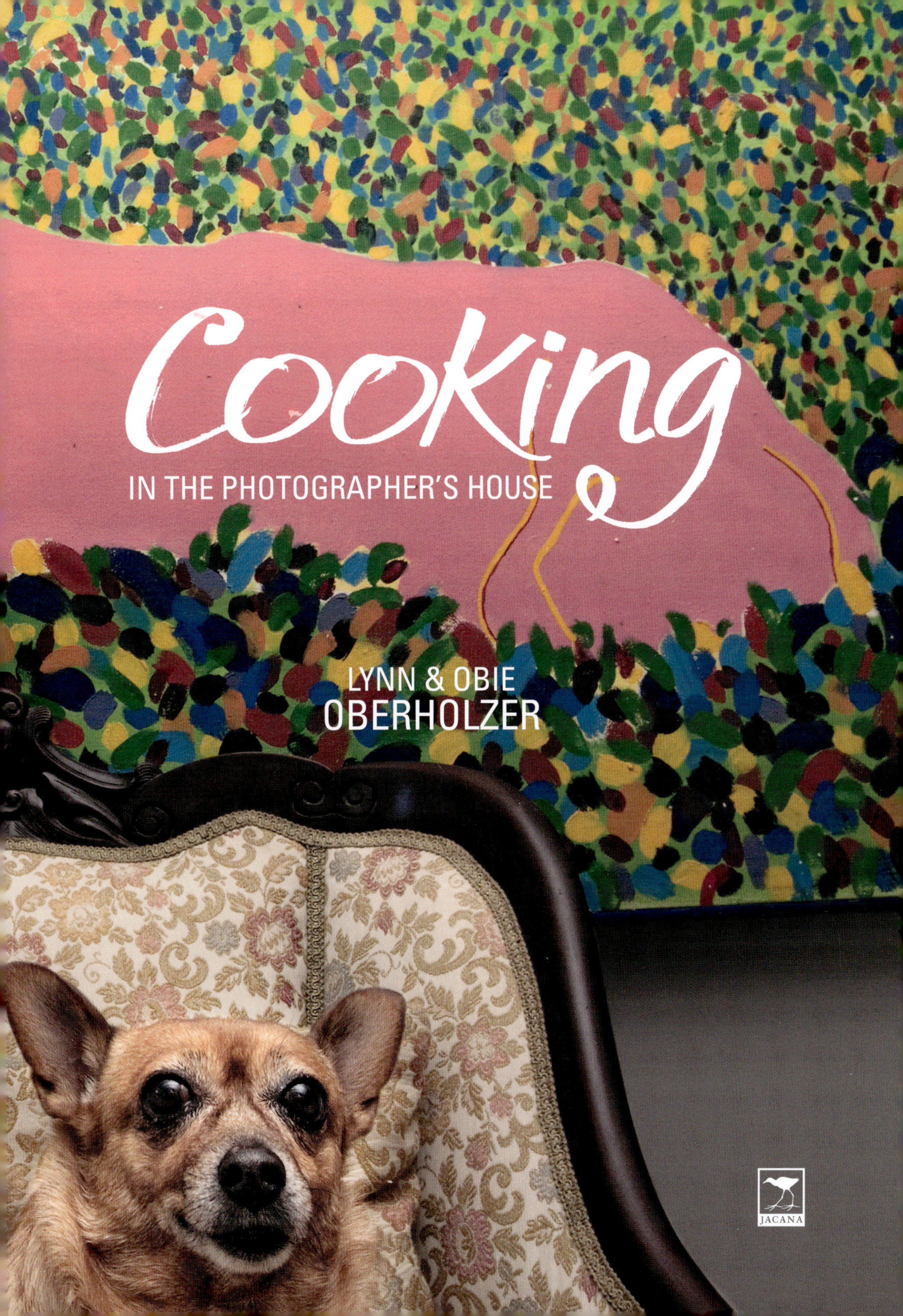
Cooking
IN THE PHOTOGRAPHER'S HOUSE
LYNN & OBIE
OBERHOLZER
JACANA

I would like to dedicate this book to the cooking parents of this world and their children. The interaction between cooking, the food on the table, the early memories of eating, and the reaction to these, form lifelong relationships to food and cooking.

I thank Obie for enjoying whatever I cook; my boys, Nic and Jesse, for the calls from all over the world asking me how to cook a certain meal; and my dear friends, who often hand over their kitchens to me when I'm visiting. This has all contributed to my love of cooking, which has never been a chore.

There are times when a single act of generosity goes beyond friendship. This is one of those times. We've come a long way since the tin-foil times on the beaches of Madagascar. Thank you Micky for believing in me; without your sponsorship this book would not have been possible.

CONTENTS

VEGETABLES & SALADS

DIPS, SPREADS & SAUCES

DESSERTS & SWEET TREATS

INTRODUCTION

I was born and raised in the countryside of KwaZulu-Natal. The fruit and vegetables we ate all came from our garden; the eggs from the hens; the milk, still warm, from the farm down the road; and the meat from our farm abattoir. We ate fish on holiday when my mom and dad fished on the Wild Coast or when the shad were running north of Durban. I remember a weekend spent camping on the beach at Salt Rock with my sister and her boyfriend. The shad were being pulled out so fast we couldn't keep up with the braaing.

Home was an old Victorian house on a big plot at the edge of the Valley of a Thousand Hills and, after a storm, an old Zulu man would trudge up the valley to bring my mom the biggest mushrooms you have ever seen. She would fry them in butter and we would believe in the magic of Nature.

My mom was proud of her French Huguenot heritage and planted everything possible: asparagus, coffee bushes, peanuts, chillies and the normal green, red, purple and orange veggies. Camperdown in the fifties and sixties was home to many Indian families, and so spices and curries also found their way into our fragrant kitchen. My dad was a butcher, and meat in all its guises featured daily on our menus. My mom made the biltong, corned beef and brawn for the butchery. There was always something happening in the kitchen to lure me inside, to distract me from the boys' games I loved playing outside. Mom was an instinctive cook, always ready to experiment. Every week, on a Thursday, her *Woman's Weekly* would arrive from England. I remember us making lasagne sheets by hand from one of the recipes, when the only pastas we had ever heard of were spaghetti bolognaise and macaroni cheese. Many years later, in the late sixties, when Obie visited for the first time, he confessed how much he loved pasta. Not prepared to make bolognaise sauce every night, she experimented with veggies and chicken, winning Obie's heart.

Sundays in Camperdown were feast days, as we never knew how many of my mom's siblings (a very close-knit group of 10) would arrive for lunch. Our 'party-line' telephone was often out of order and family and friends never bothered to ring, knowing they would be welcomed anyway. Whoever arrived always went home laden with fresh produce from the garden.

Christmas was always a huge affair with us kids running riot and the tables groaning with everything from suckling pig and turkey to puddings stuffed with tickeys and sixpences.

My father, having spent five years as a prisoner of war in Italy and Germany, was a very proud MOTH. The Moth Hall in Camperdown was the venue for most things that went on in the village. As soon as I was old enough to butter bread, I was roped in to help with catering for the many village functions held there. It was always great fun, lending a hand and listening to the women gossip and joke. I guess there are many reasons why food, for me, has always been associated with love, family, friends, fun and good times.

I love using fresh herbs, but my knowledge of them only came much later. In Camperdown we grew parsley (curly, of course) and thyme for the chicken or turkey stuffing. Obie and I lived in Germany

 | PREVIOUS SPREAD: View of Nature's Valley and the Tsitsikamma mountains from 'The Lookout'.

for three years during the early seventies, Obie studying photography and me teaching English. On our first trip to Italy we ordered fresh fish at a little seaside trattoria and were each presented with a whole fish with what looked like pine needles stuffed inside it – our first taste of rosemary. On the little Italian island of Giglio, we were astonished to find the herb growing everywhere and so started using it to liven up our camping fare. A year later, we were camping outside a little village on the Greek island of Samothraki. The very first morning, we were woken by chattering women returning from the hills, where they had been picking armfuls of oregano and sage. There was a 'cook-up' in the village square and we were invited to share the savoury goat stews cooked in big black pots on the fire – the herbs convinced me that this was the way to enrich any meal. At the 'Viktualienmarkt' in Munich, green beans were always sold with a sprig of summer savory, the herb paired with beans. As a cook, one never stops learning or experimenting. I have found that my favourite cook-ups have always been with family and friends, where everyone usually has something new to offer. My boys have taught me so much about Eastern cooking – Nic worked in a Japanese noodle restaurant, Wagamama, in London and once lived next to a Thai restaurant. He has been living in the Arab Emirates for the last seven years, where the food culture is different once again. Jesse spent many months diving in Thailand and Egypt. He now lives on the east coast of Australia and is expert at preparing seafood. Having spent their early years in a productive, catering kitchen, their relationship with food has always been intense. All of their personal experiences filtered back to my kitchen, enriching my knowledge of food.

My romance with bread started with my mother's weekly little whole-wheat loaf, which came especially for her, from an obscure baker in Durban. At that time, bread in South Africa was white and tasteless. During my Stellenbosch student years, I spent a holiday in Pretoria with Obie and his parents. His mother (a German raised in the USA) baked her own whole-wheat yeast bread. I was smitten and learnt the basics from her. On our return to South Africa after Obie's studies in Germany, in 1974, I couldn't eat our tasteless local loaves after the wonderful sourdoughs and black bread in Munich and so put myself to work learning all I could about bread baking. It was the start of a lifelong passion.

Travelling extensively in Europe during our stay there, I fell in love with the Mediterranean cuisine, dominated by olive oil, garlic and herbs. As South Africa opened up to the rest of the world in its kitchens and our farmers started cultivating olives, making cheeses and growing exotic vegetables, our taste buds lapped it up and variety became the spice of life. Now we have only to hear the name of an exotic dish and the Internet brings it into our homes. However, the tried and tested old recipes, having stood the test of time, have not been put out onto my kitchen windowsill. Rather, they have been fine-tuned and still feature on my table. The quality, texture and taste of the vegetable, the herb, the bread, the cut of meat or poultry, are what are important for me. I do not go in for sauces that drown or artificial flavours that mask the real taste of whatever it is that I am cooking. Too often, I have to remind myself that more is not always better! The Italians believe that the qualities of the raw ingredients are the start of a good meal – how can one disagree with that?

Cooking became more than just a hobby for me after our second son Jesse's birth in 1985. I certainly didn't want to go back to teaching while our boys were young. We were living in Grahamstown at that time and, because of the catering I did for Obie's exhibition openings, I was asked to cater for many university functions. This soon blossomed into a little business and I was happy to work at home and be there for my boys. I was soon asked to run a Grahamstown Festival theatre restaurant. My

PIAZZA

mom agreed to help me and so began 10 years of various festival restaurants, culminating, in the last four years, with Lynn's Trattoria. I became known for my fresh, real food, homemade bread and pasta made in full view of the clients queuing up to savour the authentic Italian taste. I must confess that I never made much profit, as I was too concerned with the quality of the food, but it was truly exhilarating, creating a short-lived, frantic restaurant, which gave pleasure to so many festivalgoers. Back then, I used Italian olive oil, which I would never do today. Now, we are blessed with a variety of local oils, which have the advantage of being fresh. You just cannot compare that freshness to oil that has travelled far and sat on numerous shelves for many months or even years!

My first experience of really fresh olive oil was in Tuscany in the early seventies, and I must admit that I was really blown away! The thick green oil, which tasted and smelt like no oil I had ever tasted before, evoked the rich beauty of the hilly Tuscan landscape. A very good friend of mine once paid for me to do an Italian cookery course in a monastery outside Florence, for which I am eternally grateful. This helped me to gain confidence and to know that I was on the right cooking path. Now, here in South Africa, we do not need to travel far to find ourselves on an olive farm. The Western Cape and parts of the Karoo produce the most deliciously fragrant oils. The joy of getting the oil fresh from the first pressing knows no bounds! I would not even consider imported oil anymore. Tokara is one of only two farms I know that bottles its oil according to the type of olive and so you can choose between the distinctive flavours of any one of Frantoio, Leccino, Mission, or a fusion of those olives. Watching the greenish oil pouring from the press is something I find particularly satisfying – an ancient food that satisfies every one of my senses. Hiking on the little Greek island of Kassos, many moons ago, we were stopped by a farmer in the hills. He invited us to enjoy his freshly picked watermelon. The day was hot and so we sat down and chatted in broken Greek and German. His son noticed my swollen arm – a spider bite – and within minutes he had grabbed a bottle of olive oil and, despite my protests, was rubbing the oil into my skin. Needless to say, by the time we had finished the melon and continued our hike to the beach we were sleeping on, the swelling had gone down and the bite was forgotten.

This cookbook is the culmination of the last forty plus years – years that Obie and I have spent together, raising our boys and five dogs. Our kitchen, as is the case in so many homes, has always been filled with love, laughter and the smell of cooking. Now that I have retired from teaching and we are living in Nature's Valley, I have had the time to work on my life-long passion. Obie needed no encouragement to work with me, thank heavens, for without his brilliance, this book would never have seen the light of day.

 NEXT SPREAD: Sunrise over the Grootrivier estuary in Nature's Valley.

PIAZZA
di San Giorgio

BREADS & BREAKFASTS

Basic Yeast Bread

This is a basic dough that can be played around with that will make 2–3 standard loaves. You can use any mixture of flours, from cake to whole-wheat. You can also add any seeds or nuts, such as linseed with whole-wheat or poppy with bread flour. After the first rising, you can shape your dough in any form – bread sticks, pizza, loaves in a tin, plaits or bread rolls. Exact quantities for bread are difficult, but once you have felt your way into the dough-making process, the pleasures and possibilities are endless. It is now possible to get stoneground flour, which improves the texture and taste of the bread. A lot of this flour is unbleached and, for me, not to be compared to the more commercial, mass-produced flours.

- 9–10 cups (2 250–2 500 ml) flour
- 4 tsp salt (omit for pizza)
- 1 litre lukewarm water
- 60 ml olive oil or butter

TIP: Oil the top of your form if doing pizza. Brush with melted butter for a soft crust when making rolls. Salted water will give a harder crust. I usually leave the dough as it is, unless I want the form shiny. Then I brush with an egg wash (beaten egg with a little water added).

- Mix all dry ingredients together, using 9 cups of flour.
- Pour water into a large mixing bowl and add oil.
- Add the dry ingredients to the water, slowly, stirring until dough is too stiff to stir.
- Start kneading and continue until you have smooth, elastic dough, adding flour to the dough if it's too sticky. Try to work as lightly as possible – you must feel your way with the 10th cup of flour.
- Shape dough into a ball and oil the outside, leaving it to rise in a warm place. Rising dough does not like to be in a cold, draughty place. I place my bowl into a plastic bag, which keeps it warmer. The rising will take about 40 minutes – the heavier the dough (depending on seeds, flour, etc), the longer it takes and the less it will rise.
- Knock the dough down, shape it into whatever form you need and let it rise again in a warm place. This will take about 30 minutes. When making rolls, you can place them close together for a decorative effect or apart for more individual rolls. Using a baking tray, you can shape any loaf you like or use a bread tin for a more conventional loaf.
- Preheat the oven to 180°C.
- A standard-size loaf will take 50 minutes, bread sticks 10 minutes, a plait 40 minutes.
- Bread rolls, if placed apart, will take 29 minutes, but allow for about 40 minutes when placed close together.
- Remove from pan and cool on a wire rack or eat immediately – there is nothing quite like freshly baked bread.

 I PREVIOUS SPREAD: Lynn running over the Grootrivier bridge in the Tsitsikamma forests.

Lynn's Whole-Wheat Bread

This was the first bread that I learnt to bake and is a very good one to start with, besides being a healthy, low-GI option. It is an adaptation of Obie's mother's recipe and will make 1 average-sized loaf.

- 5 cups whole-wheat flour
- 2 tsp salt
- 10 g (1 sachet) instant dry yeast
- 750 ml warm water
- approximately 60 ml olive oil (optional, but recommended)

- Mix all dry ingredients together in a big bowl.
- Add half of the water to the dry ingredients, mixing really well.
- Now keep adding water slowly, mixing continuously, until there is no dry flour left – you do not have to use all the water, you might even need more, depending on your flour.
- Add oil and mix again – the dough should be looking 'ropey'.
- Oil or 'Spray and Cook' a bread tin. This dough will not hold its shape as a free form.
- Spoon your dough in and flatten it – use a bit more oil to do this.
- Leave to rise in a warm place – putting your tin into a plastic grocery bag is a good idea.
- Preheat your oven to 180°C.
- When the dough reaches the top of the tin, bake for 50–60 minutes.
- Remove from tin and cool on rack. Try not to cut the bread until it has cooled a little, as it can be fragile.

Whole-Wheat Poppyseed Rusks

These rusks have been a firm family favourite, extending to friends as well, for the past 40 years. When he was little, my younger son Jesse always loved the warm, undried rusks as they came out of the oven. The original recipe, which I have adapted, came from a friend of my mother who lived in my childhood village of Camperdown in KwaZulu-Natal.

- 1½ cups brown sugar
- 1 litre buttermilk or full-cream maas (thick sour milk)
- 500g butter, melted
- 1 cup black poppyseeds
- 4 level tbsp baking powder
- 9 cups whole-wheat flour (or 8 cups of flour and 1 cup oats)

- Preheat the oven to 170°C.
- Whisk sugar and buttermilk together until combined.
- Add melted butter and whisk to combine.
- In a large mixing bowl, add the seeds and baking powder to the flour and mix well.
- Add the butter mixture and mix well to combine.
- Spray or oil 2 large, shallow oven tins (I use roasting pans, the kind you sometimes get when you buy a stove).
- Press dough evenly into the 2 tins. Wet your fingers to smooth the tops.
- Bake for 35 minutes.
- Cut into fingers and leave to cool for a while.
- Separate the fingers and place back onto the oven trays. Try not to crowd them too much – I use a third tray to prevent this.
- Dry in a 100°C oven for about 3 hours.
- Rusks keep well in an airtight container for a good 2 months.

Italian Biscotti

Can be dipped into dessert wine or coffee. This will be sufficient for 6–8 people, but I always double up on this recipe as they keep so well.

- 125g butter at room temperature
- ¾ cup (190ml) castor sugar
- 3 free-range eggs
- 2 tbsp brandy
- 1 tbsp grated lemon rind
- 1½ cups (375ml) bread flour
- ¾ cup (190ml) self-raising flour
- ½ tsp salt
- 125g roasted almonds or any other nuts, roughly chopped
- 1 tbsp aniseed (optional – it gives a very specific flavour, so don't use unless you really like it)

TIP: You can get away with not roasting the almonds beforehand. I have used walnuts and hazelnuts instead of almonds.

- Preheat the oven to 180°C.
- Cream butter and sugar.
- Add eggs, one at a time, beating well.
- Add brandy and lemon rind.
- Add flours and salt. Mix well.
- Stir in almonds and aniseed, if using.
- Cover dough and refrigerate for at least one hour.
- Using a sprinkling of flour, roll pieces of dough into sausage shapes, 2–3 cm thick.
- Place on greased oven tray with 4cm in-between the rolls.
- Bake for 20 minutes until light brown.
- Cut diagonally while still hot, about 1½ cm thick.
- Separate pieces and dry out in the oven at 100°C until properly dry. This will take about 2 hours.
- Store the biscotti in an airtight container and they will last at least 2 months, if you can resist them!

Breakfast Oats

I am a firm believer in the nutritional value of oats. Added to that, its low-GI content keeps us happily satisfied until lunchtime. This recipe is one that I thought up during the summer when cooked oats was not an appropriate breakfast.

- 200 ml raw rolled oats (I use the blue box of Tiger Oats)
- sufficient milk to cover the oats, plus a little extra
- fresh fruit: berries, figs, pomegranates (in summer) and grated apple or diced pear (in winter)
- dried fruit: cranberries or raisins
- nuts: almonds or walnuts
- a sprinkling of cinnamon

- Soak the oats in the milk overnight in the fridge – if you are lactose intolerant, you can soak the oats in fruit juice.
- Add the fresh fruit.
- Sprinkle with the cranberries or raisins to add sweetness, and the nuts.
- Finish off with a good sprinkle of cinnamon and you have the most satisfying breakfast ever.
- If, like us, you are a milk lover, add some extra milk.

Sit outside if possible and enjoy, knowing that you are giving your body the best possible start to the day.

 NEXT SPREAD: Moon rise over the Blue Rocks at Nature's Valley and farewell to long analogue time exposures.

TOKARA

SOUPS

Wholesome Chicken Soup

Everyone should have a chicken soup recipe. It is the ultimate comfort food, besides containing all you need for your health and 'feel-good happiness'. If you start off with my recipe, you can make your own changes according to your likes and dislikes.

- 1 free-range chicken, any size
- 4 litres of water
- 1 tin chopped Italian tomatoes
- 3 onions, roughly diced
- 3 leeks, sliced finely, green part included
- 5 cloves garlic, crushed roughly
- 2 thumbnails of fresh ginger, peeled and sliced thinly
- 4 stalks of celery, sliced finely, with the leaves
- 5 carrots, each one cut into 3 pieces
- 5 medium-sized potatoes, cut into big chunks
- 6–8 baby marrows, sliced roughly
- 8 (approximately) mushrooms, sliced
- herbs: fresh rosemary, sage, thyme, parsley (be generous, but go easy on the rosemary as it can dominate)
- spices: 1 tsp each of cumin, paprika, turmeric
- a few threads of saffron
- salt and ground black pepper to taste

- Place everything in a large pot. Bring to the boil and simmer gently for a good hour, until the chicken starts falling off the bone.
- Remove the chicken, debone it, cut up all the meat, give the skin to the dog and put as much chicken back into the soup as you like.
- Check the seasoning.

Serve with crusty bread.

TIP: I sometimes keep some chicken apart for a salad the next day.

Barley and Bean Soup

This is a basic recipe that can be adapted according to the dried pulses or veggies you have on hand.

- 2 large onions
- 3 cloves garlic
- 2 carrots
- 3 sticks celery, green and all
- butter or oil for frying
- 125 g smoked ham or bacon
- ½ cup (125 ml) barley
- 1 cup (250 ml) dried butter beans
- 8 cups (2 litres) vegetable stock
- salt and ground black pepper to taste
- fresh thyme, parsley and sage to taste, finely chopped
- ¼ cup (60 ml) cream (optional)

- Chop vegetables finely and fry briefly in butter or oil.
- Stir in ham or bacon.
- Add barley, beans and hot stock.
- Bring to boil and simmer for about 2 hours, until barley and beans are soft.
- Season and add herbs and cream (if using).

Serve with homemade bread.

Split Pea and Bacon Soup

Obie and I were really cold this last winter and so this was one of the hearty soups I came up with in an attempt to warm and comfort us. It will be enough for 4 people as a main meal.

- 6 leeks, sliced thinly, white and green included
- 1 red onion, diced
- 250 g smoked back bacon, sliced (or smoked ribs)
- olive oil for frying
- 4 cloves garlic, crushed
- freshly ground black pepper
- 1 tsp sweet paprika
- 10 cups (2 500 ml) water with appropriate amount vegetable stock powder
- 4 celery stalks, sliced thinly, leaves included
- 1 large carrot, diced
- 1 turnip, diced
- 4 baby marrows, diced
- 1 pkt green split peas
- 3 bay leaves
- fresh herbs to taste: oregano, thyme, sage, parsley
- salt to taste
- 1 bunch spinach (Swiss chard), large stalks removed, cut small

- Fry the leeks, onion and bacon in a little olive oil. Add garlic.
- As the onion softens, add the pepper and paprika. Stir briefly.
- Add your stock plus all veggies and dried peas, but not the spinach.
- Bring to the boil. Add bay leaves and herbs.
- Simmer until peas are mushy – about 40 minutes.
- Add salt to taste.
- Add fresh spinach.
- Bring back to boil and simmer for 10 minutes.

Serve with freshly baked seed bread for a wholesome meal.

TIP: I always use fresh herbs, so I use a lot more than you would if you have to resort to dried ones, which are more powerful.

Chunky Mushroom Soup

This is my friend Jenny's soup recipe, which we used when she came up to Grahamstown to lend a hand during the chaotic Grahamstown Festival. It is different and really chunky.

- 4 tbsp butter
- 3 tbsp flour
- 2½ cups chicken stock (625 ml)
- 400 ml milk
- 500 g mushrooms, cleaned (wipe, don't rinse), roughly chopped
- 30 ml fresh lemon juice (juice of one lemon)
- salt and ground black pepper to taste
- 150 ml cream
- 200 ml dry sherry or port
- Italian parsley – lots

- Melt butter in a heavy-bottomed pot.
- Using a whisk, add flour. When absorbed, add stock slowly, whisking all the time.
- Add milk, stirring until you have a thick, smooth sauce.
- Add mushrooms, lemon juice and pepper.
- Bring to the boil and taste for salt.
- Add sherry, cream and parsley.

Serve piping hot with fresh rolls or crusty bread.

TIP: This soup must not cook for long – the mushrooms should remain firm.

OPINEL
INOX

Fresh Tomato Soup

- 2 large onions, finely diced
- 1 potato, finely chopped
- olive oil for frying
- 5 ml sweet paprika
- 2 ml ground cumin (optional)
- 1½ kg very ripe tomatoes, chopped (tinned tomatoes can also be used)
- 2 sticks of celery, finely sliced, green included
- 500 ml vegetable or chicken stock
- salt and ground black pepper to taste
- a handful of fresh basil or parsley, finely chopped
- fresh Parmesan (optional)
- sour cream (optional)

- Fry onions and potato in olive oil with the spices, cover the pot and simmer until cooked, stirring frequently to prevent potato from sticking.
- Add tomatoes, celery, hot stock and salt and pepper, and simmer for a further 10 minutes.
- The soup is done and you can either blend it smooth or leave it chunky.
- Serve hot or chilled with sprinkles of basil or parsley.
- Grated fresh Parmesan is good if the soup is hot.
- A swirl of fresh or sour cream is good hot or cold.

TIP: I prefer to use tinned tomatoes when I cannot get really ripe organic tomatoes.

EN FABRIKANT, GAAN
WINKEL
zware
repen
108
Delicata chocolade

Island Fish Soup

This is my basic fish soup recipe. The quality of the stock is important, so try to get extra fish heads for your stock.

STOCK
- fish heads
- 2 litres cold water
- onion, coarsely chopped
- carrot, coarsely chopped
- a few threads of saffron
- 2 bay leaves
- 5 ml turmeric
- salt and ground black pepper to taste

SOUP
- 1 kg filleted white fish
- salt and ground black pepper to taste
- 1 lemon
- 60 ml olive oil
- 4 onions, chopped
- 4 ripe tomatoes, finely chopped (or 1 tin)
- 3 medium potatoes, peeled and chopped smallish
- 3 cloves garlic, crushed
- herbs: fresh parsley, lemon thyme, fennel or dill

TIP: Mussels or any other seafood, such as prawns, can be added to make this soup special.

STOCK
- If you are making your own stock, put all of the bits and pieces that you can get from the fish shop – heads, bones, etc – into a big pot of water.
- Add remaining ingredients.
- Bring to the boil and simmer for 30 minutes.
- Leave to cool and strain.
- Remove all flesh from the head and bones to add to the soup.

SOUP
- Fry the fish gently in a little olive oil, until just cooked, turning once.
- Season with salt, pepper and a squeeze of lemon. Put aside.
- Heat oil in a big pot and stir-fry all soup ingredients (except fried fish) for 15 minutes.
- Add fish stock, bring to the boil and simmer until the potatoes are done.
- Add fried fish, breaking it into chunks.
- Taste for salt and heat through – you don't want the fish to cook any more.
- Chop fresh herbs and sprinkle onto soup.

Serve with chopped parsley and a spoonful of sour cream. A good bread is essential for optimal enjoyment.

MAINS

Baked Fresh Fish

Fresh fish is at its best if left whole and roasted to perfection in the oven. For those who love the taste of fish, this is the ultimate taste sensation.

- fresh fish, cleaned and gutted
- olive oil, for coating
- fresh rosemary
- 1–2 lemons, for slicing and the juice
- coarse sea salt

- Preheat the oven to 200°C.
- Coat the fish with olive oil, put fresh rosemary in the cavity with a few slices of lemon and sprinkle with coarse sea salt.
- Bake for about 20 minutes – time will depend on the size of the fish, but you do not want to overcook it. When the flesh flakes easily and is white, it's done.
- Squeeze fresh lemon over the fish as it comes out of the oven and serve immediately.

TIP: In days gone by, Obie did a lot of spear fishing. We sometimes did the fish on the coals, which was also good. On a trip to Madagascar with friends in 1975, we camped on the east coast. Obie and Gerrit shot fish every day and we cooked them on the coals in tin foil, until our tin foil was stolen. This meant that we had to do without it, but it was a blessing in disguise. The increase in flavour without the foil was remarkable. I have never used foil for fish again.

My younger son Jesse says you should never add fresh lemon juice before cooking as this in itself cooks the fish – you can marinate it in lemon if your fish is fresh and then you won't need to cook it at all! We did this once with a Japanese hitchhiker and simply dipped the marinated fish into soya sauce. This was of course before we had discovered the tastiness of raw fish.

 | PREVIOUS SPREAD: Lynn running on Nature's Valley beach.

Basic Italian-Style Risotto

This is a very basic risotto, which can be flavoured in many different ways. You need time to do this properly, so no short cuts! Quantities are really not important, but you do need sufficient stock.

- 2 onions, finely chopped
- 1 carrot, finely chopped
- 1 stick celery, finely chopped
- olive oil for frying
- 2 cloves garlic, finely chopped
- 100g Arborio rice per person
- dry wine or Vermouth
- good quality stock (prepare appropriately for the optional addition of meat, fish, chicken, etc.)
- meat, fish, free-range chicken or veggies (depending on what risotto you are making – all pre-cooked)
- salt and ground black pepper to taste
- 1 heaped tbsp butter (don't stint here, it does make a difference)
- Parmesan, freshly grated
- lots of parsley, freshly chopped

- Fry the vegetables in plenty of olive oil in a good-sized, heavy-bottomed pot.
- Add garlic and rice and stir-fry until well coated with oil.
- Keep the premade stock hot next to the rice pot.
- Start adding the wine and the stock, a little at a time, stirring continuously – as the rice absorbs the stock, you add more. The rice should be only just covered by the hot stock.
- Continue until the rice is cooked. A good risotto has a mushy look to it, but the rice grains must not disintegrate.
- Add your meat, fish, chicken or veggies, and let it heat through.
- Now add the butter, Parmesan and parsley.
- Risotto should be served and eaten immediately, although leftovers soon disappear from my fridge.

TIP: My favourite risotto is chicken, so I make a thin chicken soup using a whole chicken, 2 onions, 4 stalks of celery and 2 carrots. I use the soup as my stock and dice the cooked chicken to add at the end, or else keep it to use in a salad.

Thai-Style Green Curry

- 2 onions, sliced
- olive oil, for frying
- 3 free-range chicken breasts (or 1 pork fillet), cut into strips
- 2 tbsp green curry paste (this can vary according to taste)
- 1 tsp ground cumin
- 4 cardamom pods, roughly crushed
- ground black pepper
- veggies: 1 chopped aubergine, 3 sliced baby marrows, 1 sliced red/yellow pepper, handful of cauliflower florets (these are my favourites, but use what you have)
- 1 tin coconut cream or milk (you may only need half, unless you can get the cute baby tins)
- 3 cloves garlic, crushed
- 1 knob ginger, crushed or sliced
- 2 tsp brown sugar or honey (optional)
- 2 tbsp oyster sauce
- 2 tbsp soya sauce
- 1 tsp fish sauce
- 1 stalk lemon grass, crushed with a knife handle
- salt to taste
- fresh coriander

- Stir-fry onions until just starting to brown.
- Add chicken or pork, curry paste, cumin, cardamom and black pepper.
- Stir-fry over high heat to seal.
- Add veggies, fry for about 3 minutes.
- Add all the remaining ingredients, keeping the coriander as a garnish.
- Simmer gently until the meat is done – do not overcook.

Serve with rice, noodles or butternut. If using eastern noodles, precook them according to instructions on the packet and add them to the stir-fry with the coriander at the end. If serving with rice or roast butternut, serve separately.

S BOTTLE
S THE
OPERTY OF
THE
H AFRICA
WERIES

Chicken Casserole

This is a basic recipe, which calls for any other innovative ideas you might like to add. I like to cook chicken with the skin as this does increase the flavour.

- 1 free-range chicken, cut into pieces (or chicken pieces)
- olive oil for browning
- 4 onions, roughly chopped
- 6 cloves garlic, roughly chopped
- 2 thumbnails of fresh ginger, peeled and sliced thinly
- 1 tsp each of ground cumin, sweet paprika, turmeric, ground coriander, ground black pepper, salt
- 4 stalks celery, chopped fine, including the leaves
- 4 large carrots, each cut into 3 pieces
- other veggies: red pepper (roughly cut), whole baby marrow
- 2 cups (500 ml) dry red wine, heated
- a handful of fresh herbs: thyme, sage, rosemary, parsley (use less rosemary than the other 3 and remove stalks)

- Preheat the oven to 170°C.
- Using a large ovenproof casserole with a lid, brown the chicken pieces in olive oil, removing them as they brown.
- Brown the onion, garlic and ginger with the spices. As the onion browns, add the rest of the vegetables. When they have fried a while, add the chicken pieces and the red wine.
- Bring everything to the boil. Add the herbs and place into the oven with the lid on. Cook for 1½ hours.

Serve with healthy quinoa, brown rice or lentils. For those of you not eating carbs, roast butternut is my first choice. You will not miss the rice! Homemade bread is good to mop up the juices.

TIP: You could cook this on top of the stove, but the oven seems to give a better result.

Flattened Roast Chicken

- 1 whole free-range chicken
- sprinkling of olive oil
- 20 ml fresh lemon juice
- 1 tbsp each of fresh rosemary, thyme, sage, parsley (all finely chopped)
- 1 tsp each of ground cumin, sweet paprika, ground coriander, turmeric, coarse salt and coarse black pepper
- dried chilli flakes (optional)
- 1 onion, quartered
- choice of vegetables to roast: potato wedges, diced butternut, halved red peppers, whole mushrooms, whole baby marrows, ripe tomatoes (halved, cut-side up)

- Preheat the oven to 200°C.
- Flatten the chicken by cutting down the breast side and opening up.
- Press down hard in the middle of the chicken with the skin-side up.
- Using your hands, oil both sides of the chicken.
- Pour over the lemon juice.
- Season both sides with the herbs and spices.
- Oil a baking tray and place chicken, skin side up, on top of the onion.
- Roast for 50 minutes.
- I usually roast the veggies at the same time – using your hands, oil them and season with salt and pepper.
- This is a quick way to feed about 5 people, with everything going into the oven at the same time. Some of the veggies will not take as long as the chicken, so keep checking the mushrooms, baby marrows and tomatoes.

Chicken Filo Pie

This is a traditional Greek pie, which is an ideal party dish as you can do everything well before the time.

STOCK
- 1 whole free-range chicken (about 1½ kg)
- 1 large onion, roughly chopped
- 2 bay leaves
- 2 tbsp mixed fresh sage, thyme, rosemary and parsley
- 1 tsp ground paprika
- salt and ground black pepper to taste
- 2 large onions, chopped
- 2 sticks celery, chopped

SAUCE
- 3 tbsp butter
- 5 tbsp flour
- ½ cup milk
- 2 cups stock (from above)
- 4 free-range eggs, beaten
- a bunch of fresh parsley, chopped

PIE FILLING
- 2 large onions, roughly chopped
- 3–4 sticks celery, sliced, green and all
- 3 cloves garlic, crushed

PASTRY
- 250 g filo pastry
- olive oil, for brushing

STOCK
- Put all of the stock ingredients into a big pot and only just cover with water.
- Bring to the boil and simmer for an hour, by which time the chicken should be cooked through.
- Cool chicken in the stock and then remove. Keep for the filling.
- Boil the stock to reduce – you will need about 2 cups.

SAUCE
- Melt the butter and stir in the flour.
- Add the milk and 2 cups stock – this should be a thick sauce.
- Add eggs and parsley. Mix everything together.
- Check seasoning.

PIE FILLING / PASTRY
- Preheat the oven at 180°C.
- Debone and dice the chicken.
- Fry onions, celery and garlic until cooked. Add to the chicken.
- Choose a shallow oven dish and layer half of the filo, brushing each layer with olive oil.
- Spoon in the chicken and layer the other half of the filo on top, brushing each layer with olive oil.
- Bake for 40 minutes.

I serve a fresh salad of chopped cucumber, tomato and onion with this pie. Freshly baked bread, for those still eating carbs, is a tasty addition.

TIP: If the dish you are using can fit into your freezer, you can freeze it before baking. Defrost overnight or for the day and bake as directed.

HAMILTONS
60mm
PURE BRISTLE

Baked Aubergine with Mince and Pine Nuts

This is my most recent discovery – the aubergine just melts in your mouth.

- 4 medium aubergines, sliced lengthways
- 90 ml olive oil (Tokara Mission is ideal)
- 1½ tsp ground cumin
- 1½ tsp ground sweet paprika
- 1 tbsp ground cinnamon (this gives the mince a completely different taste, almost completing the fullness)
- 2 medium onions, finely chopped
- 500 g lean beef mince (or lamb mince)
- 3 cloves garlic, crushed
- 2 sticks celery, green and all, finely chopped
- 50 g pine nuts
- 4 tsp (20 ml) tomato purée
- 1 bunch parsley, finely chopped
- 140 ml water
- 4 cinnamon sticks
- 4 bay leaves
- 60 ml fresh lemon juice
- salt and ground black pepper to taste

- Preheat the oven to 200°C.
- Place aubergines cut-side up, in an oiled roasting tin. Brush cut sides liberally with olive oil, sprinkle with salt and pepper and roast for 20 minutes. Remove and cool.
- In the meanwhile, start the mince mixture by heating some olive oil in a large pan.
- Mix the cumin, paprika and cinnamon. Add half the spice mix to the heated pan along with the onions. Stir-fry for a while before adding the mince, garlic, celery, pine nuts, tomato purée, salt and black pepper.
- Continue cooking until the mince is cooked and then add the parsley.
- Place the remaining spice mix in a bowl and add the water, cinnamon sticks, bay leaves and a good pinch of salt and lemon juice. Mix well.
- Reduce your oven temperature to 180°C. Pour the spice mix into the bottom of the pan in which your aubergines are resting. Spoon the mince mixture carefully onto the aubergines. Cover the tin tightly with foil and return to the oven for 1½ hours.
- You can baste the aubergines during the baking period, but I only do it at the end and they are perfect.

Serve with fresh bread, a crunchy cucumber and tomato salad or a simple green vegetable.

Whole Fillet with a Crust

This was how my mom roasted a fillet. The crust seems to keep the flavour in, with the mustard complimenting the richness of the beef.

- 1 whole beef fillet, any size, depending on how many people you are feeding
- 2 cloves garlic, cut into slivers
- 3 tbsp whole-wheat flour
- 1 tbsp English mustard powder
- 1 tbsp coarse salt
- 1 tbsp brown sugar (nowadays, I omit the sugar)

- Using the sharp point of a knife, insert garlic into fillet.
- Place all dry ingredients into a clean plastic bag.
- Put the fillet into the bag, shaking it around to cover it with the crust. Wrap it up tightly and leave to stand for a few hours or overnight.
- Preheat the oven to 220°C.
- Oil an oven dish for the fillet and pack any loose crust onto the meat.
- Roast open for 30 minutes. The timing will depend on how you like your fillet, but the crust does protect the meat and I always find that it takes 10 minutes longer than it would without the crust.
- Rest for 10 minutes before slicing – delicious hot or cold.

Bobotie

This is a South African dish introduced to this country by Malay immigrants. I have used this particular recipe for the last 30-odd years. I recently made it in the Netherlands for a group of Dutch and American friends. It was an instant hit.

- fruit: 60g dried apricots, 60g dried apple, 60g raisins
- 2½cm slice of bread
- 450ml milk
- 500g lean steak mince
- 1tbsp butter
- 2 large onions, diced
- 1tbsp curry powder, mild or hot
- 30ml vinegar
- 2tsp salt
- ½tsp black pepper
- 2tbsp sugar
- 2½tbsp chutney
- 2 free-range eggs
- 6 lemon leaves
- 6 bay leaves
- 12 almonds, chopped

- Soak the fruit overnight in cold water just covered, and then chop fine. Keep the water.
- Preheat the oven to 160°C.
- Soak bread in 150ml of the milk, mash and add to the mince in a bowl.
- Melt butter and sauté onion.
- Add curry powder and fry.
- Add the fruit mixture and water to the pan with the vinegar, salt, pepper, sugar and chutney.
- Simmer until thick and then mash.
- Add to mince mixture, stirring well.
- Place in a buttered baking dish.
- Whisk eggs with remaining milk. Pour over meat, sprinkle with leaves and almonds.
- Bake for about one hour, until set.

Serve with yellow rice (cook rice with turmeric and raisins). Sambals of chutney, desiccated coconut and sliced banana go well with this bobotie.

Traditional Lasagne

This was the lasagne (beef) I made for my Grahamstown Festival trattoria. Served with a fresh salad, it pleases most palates. The beef can be substituted with chicken or lentils.

- 2 onions, diced
- 1 carrot, diced
- 2 sticks celery, sliced thinly, with the green
- 3 rashers bacon (optional)
- olive oil
- 350g lean minced beef (or 350g minced chicken or 350g cooked brown lentils)
- 100g chicken livers (optional)
- 4tbsp dry white wine
- 1 tin chopped Italian tomatoes
- 1tbsp tomato paste
- 2tbsp chopped, fresh oregano
- salt and ground black pepper to taste
- ground sweet paprika to taste
- 225g lasagna sheets

- WHITE SAUCE
- 40g butter
- 40g flour
- 600ml milk
- nutmeg
- grated Parmesan to sprinkle on top

- Preheat the oven to 180°C.
- Fry vegetables and bacon in olive oil for a few minutes, add beef or chicken. Stir-fry to brown meat.
- Add livers and brown them.
- Add wine, tomatoes, paste, herbs and seasoning. Simmer until the sauce has thickened.
- If using lentils, add the cooked lentils to the vegetable sauce once it has thickened.
- Meanwhile, make a white sauce by melting the butter, whisk in the flour, slowly add the milk, whisking continuously until sauce thickens. This sauce must not be too thick – must be easy pouring.
- Assemble the lasagne in an appropriate oven dish. Start with the meat, lentils or chicken in a layer. Place the lasagne sheets, covering the meat but not overlapping. Cover with white sauce in a thin layer, and then repeat. You should end with a liberal amount of white sauce on top. Sprinkle with Parmesan and bake for 40 minutes.

327
Schleißheimer Str

Greek Moussaka

This is an old, traditional recipe that I used extensively during my catering days. One Grahamstown Festival, I ran a Greek taverna and this moussaka was a real hit.

MOUSSAKA
- 3 aubergines (about 1½ kg), 2 sliced and 1 cubed
- 50 ml flour
- 100 ml olive oil
- 4 onions, diced
- 1 kg lean minced beef (or lamb mince if you can get it)
- 1 tin tomatoes
- 2 cloves garlic, crushed
- 1 tbsp fresh oregano, chopped
- 2 ml ground cinnamon
- 1 tin tomato purée
- 75 ml Parmesan, grated
- salt and ground black pepper to taste

SAUCE
- 30 g flour
- 750 ml milk
- 3 free-range eggs
- salt and ground black pepper to taste
- 30 g butter

MOUSSAKA
- Preheat the oven to 160°C.
- Dredge the aubergine slices in flour and fry in olive oil.
- Remove from pan and sauté the onions.
- Add the mince and cubed aubergine and continue frying until mince is brown.
- Add the tomatoes, herbs and spices, and purée and simmer to reduce most of the liquid.
- Now make the sauce – see below.
- Layer half the mince in a shallow oven dish, cover with the aubergine slices, layer the rest of the mince and top with the sauce.
- Sprinkle with Parmesan and bake for 30 minutes. Then turn the oven up to 200°C for a further 15 minutes.

SAUCE
- In a bowl, blend flour with a little milk. Add eggs, salt and pepper.
- Heat the remaining milk and butter until bubbles appear.
- Add egg mixture slowly, stirring until thick and boiling.

Serve with a fresh salad of chopped cucumber, tomatoes, feta cheese and onion.

Lamb Curry

This is the basic curry recipe, which I grew up with. We always used fresh curry paste, which my mom would buy from an Indian family in Camperdown. Unless you make curry very often, it's not worth keeping too many spices you do not use regularly. I prefer using a paste, but have made good curries with curry powder. I have used butternut and aubergine, whereas the original recipe used potatoes – the choice is yours. I often omit the butternut and then serve it separately with the curry instead of rice.

- 6 onions, roughly chopped
- oil for frying
- 4–6 tsp red curry paste (or follow instructions on whatever curry spice you have – Packo makes a good one)
- spices: curry leaves, cinnamon stick, star anise, fennel seeds, mustard seeds
- 2 fresh chillies (optional)
- 2 bay leaves
- 1 kg lamb knuckles (sliced lamb shanks)
- 5 cloves garlic, crushed
- 4 pieces of 'hazelnut-sized' fresh ginger, peeled and crushed
- 4–6 diced fresh tomatoes (or a tin of tomatoes)
- ½ butternut, cubed
- 2 aubergines, cubed and peeled
- 1 tbsp honey (optional)
- fresh coriander leaves

- Fry onions in canola or olive oil.
- Add curry paste, crushed seeds, chillies and other spices – fry gently.
- Add lamb, garlic and ginger and brown the lamb.
- Add tomato, bring to the boil and then lower the temperature.
- Simmer with a closed lid for 1 hour and then add the butternut, aubergine and honey.
- Simmer for another hour, by which time the lamb should be soft.
- Let the curry stand for 10 minutes. Scoop off any excess oil.
- Add the coriander leaves.

Serve with brown basmati rice or roast butternut. Optional extras are chutney, tzatziki (especially if your curry is very hot) and sliced banana in yoghurt.

TIP: My mom always made a diced tomato and onion salad with lemon juice. Add extra sliced chilli in lemon juice or vinegar for the chilli-lovers!

Lamb Shanks

This is old-fashioned comfort food at its best!

- 6 lamb shanks – one per person or ½ each for ladies if very big (the shanks, that is!)
- coarse sea salt, ground black pepper, ground cumin and ground paprika
- 2 tbsp olive oil
- 6 onions, peeled and coarsely chopped
- 2 tbsp finely chopped fresh rosemary
- 300 ml dry red wine
- 175 ml balsamic vinegar

TIP: Ox-tail can be done in the same way, using beer instead of wine and oregano instead of the rosemary. I have also done ostrich neck with this recipe – very successfully.

- Preheat the oven to 200°C.
- Toss the lamb in the spices.
- Using a heavy oven pot with a lid, heat the oil, brown the shanks and remove them from the pot.
- Fry the onions briefly, add the rosemary and garlic for a minute, then add the wine and vinegar.
- Put the lamb back into the pot and heat until boiling.
- Put the lid on and transfer to the oven – turn the oven down to 170°C and bake for 2–2½ hours until the meat is falling off the bone. Check from time to time, basting and adding more wine if the sauce dries up.
- You can add carrots and potatoes for the last hour if you want a one-pot meal.

Serve with vegetables of your choice. A friend of mine Linny Badenhorst adds fresh whole quinces for the last hour – a truly delicious accompaniment!

NAMIBIA

Rosemary Lamb Casserole

- 1 deboned leg of lamb, with meat cubed (keep the bone)

MARINADE

- 2tbsp fresh rosemary, shredded
- 12 peppercorns, crushed
- 12 juniper berries, crushed
- 2 onions, roughly chopped
- 8 cloves garlic, crushed
- 250ml dry red wine
- 60ml olive oil
- juice of 1 lemon

CASSEROLE

- 20 whole pickling onions
- olive oil
- 5 cloves of garlic, roughly crushed
- 1 bottle beer (or 300ml water), heated
- leg bone
- salt to taste
- veggies: lightly cooked or steamed such as green beans, carrots, aubergine, baby marrows

MARINADE

- Combine all of the ingredients and marinate the lamb overnight or up to 3 days.
- Drain the lamb in a colander, reserving the marinade.

CASSEROLE

- Preheat the oven to 160°C.
- Using an oven casserole with a lid, brown the onions lightly in a little olive oil and then remove.
- Brown the drained meat in the same pot. Add the onions, garlic, beer, marinade liquid and the bone. Add salt to taste.
- Cover the casserole and place in the oven for about 3 hours.
- Check halfway through and add more water / beer if necessary.
- Add veggies if using and heat through (adding at the end ensures that they are not overcooked).

Serve with brown rice, couscous, quinoa or roast butternut.

Roast Leg of Lamb

When I was a student at Stellenbosch, my home from home was the farm Knorhoek. Tannie Myra and Oom Hannes were my surrogate parents. Tannie Myra was, like most farmers' wives, a wonderful cook and her long dining-room table was the scene of many a loud Sunday lunch, ringing with laughter, a happy gathering of family and students. She did her roasts in this way – memories one can taste.

- 1 leg of lamb
- 2 cloves garlic, cut into slivers
- olive oil
- fresh rosemary or oregano
- salt and ground black pepper to taste
- some red wine

TIP: This is a roast and the lamb will be slightly pink. It is not a 'fall off the bone', slow-cooked lamb.

- Preheat the oven to 220°C.
- Using the sharp point of a knife, insert garlic into lamb.
- Rub the lamb with olive oil and sprinkle with the herbs and seasoning. Place in an open roasting pan, which has been oiled. Pour a little red wine into the pan, just enough to cover the bottom.
- Roast for 20 minutes.
- Turn oven down to 180°C and roast a further 80–100 minutes, depending on the size of the leg.
- Rest the roast for 10 minutes before carving as thinly as you can.
- Place the carved lamb back into the roasting pan to mingle with the juices.

Serve with fresh seasonal vegetables, lightly cooked. Tannie Myra always served homemade cream cheese piled into peach halves (homemade, bottled, yellow-cling peaches) to compliment the roast.

 | PREVIOUS SPREAD: Lynn near the cliffs at the end of Nature's Valley beach.

Pork Stir-Fry

Pork fillet has no fat, so for those of you avoiding fat, it is the ideal meat. This recipe can be made with chicken breasts instead of pork – equally delicious.

- 500g pork fillet, cut into strips
- 3tbsp (45ml) oyster sauce
- juice of ½ lemon
- canola oil
- sesame oil
- 1 onion, sliced
- 4 cloves garlic, crushed
- 1 red chilli, sliced (optional)
- 1 thumbnail of fresh ginger, sliced finely
- 3 medium carrots, cut into short strips
- 1 red pepper, cut into strips
- 1 baby red cabbage, sliced finely
- 4 brown mushrooms, sliced
- 1tbsp (15ml) fish sauce
- 3tbsp (45ml) soya sauce

- Marinate the pork in the oyster sauce and lemon juice for 30 minutes or more. This is the way that my son Jesse does it and the marinating does make a difference. Stir-fry pork in a little canola oil with a dash of sesame oil.
- Remove when brown.
- Stir-fry the onion with the garlic, chilli and ginger.
- Add the carrot, red pepper and cabbage.
- Add the mushrooms.
- The secret is not to overcook the vegetables. You want them to be a little crunchy.
- When the veg is almost done, add the fish sauce and soya sauce.
- Add the cooked pork and stir-fry to amalgamate the flavours.

Serve with rice noodles, or brown basmati rice. Have extra soya sauce on the table. No salt is necessary as the fish sauce is very salty.

New Year Lentils with Spanish Sausage

An Italian friend of mine, Christina Franco, taught me that in order to have a prosperous year, one must eat lentils every New Year's Eve or New Year's Day. This recipe has become my offering to the gods who control the Oberholzer's finances.

- 1 pkt brown lentils, or green if available
- 2 onions, diced
- olive oil
- 4 cloves garlic, crushed
- 1 thumbnail of ginger, peeled and sliced
- 5 ml ground cumin
- 5 ml ground paprika
- 1 red chilli (optional)
- 2 stalks of celery, thinly sliced with the leaves
- 2 carrots, diced
- 1 tin Italian tomatoes, diced
- 1 tbsp tomato paste
- 1 tbsp each of fresh sage and thyme, chopped
- salt and ground black pepper to taste
- 1 Chorizo sausage, about 30-cm long, or smaller ones to make up the length
- fresh coriander or parsley, finely chopped, to garnish

- Cook lentils as per instructions, not too soft, as they will cook a while in the stew.
- Stir-fry the onions in a little olive oil. Add the garlic, ginger, spices and then the vegetables.
- Add tomatoes and paste with the herbs and simmer to reduce a bit and cook the vegetables.
- Check the seasoning.
- Add the sausage, sliced, and the lentils. Once the lentils are cooked through, you are due for a prosperous new year – happy happy! Don't forget the garnish.

Ostrich Mince Frikkadels

I often use ostrich mince instead of beef mince. It makes ideal patties, as it seems to bind better than beef.

- 500g fresh ostrich, beef or lamb mince
- 1 onion, finely chopped
- 3tbsp oats, soaked briefly in a little boiling water (optional)
- 2 extra-large free-range eggs, beaten with a fork
- 1 stick of celery, sliced very finely
- 1 medium carrot, grated
- 1 thumbnail of fresh ginger, grated
- 4 cloves garlic, crushed
- 1 red chilli, sliced finely
- 4tbsp fresh herbs of your choice (thyme, oregano, sage, parsley) – I like to use a combination
- 1tsp ground sweet paprika
- sprinkling of turmeric and cumin
- ground black pepper
- 1tsp salt

- Combine everything in a bowl. Start by using a fork and then get your hands in.
- Using your hands, make any sized patties – flat, round or cigar shaped.
- Shape them well, placing them on a plate to rest a while. I often leave them in the fridge overnight at this stage.
- You can either shallow-fry your frikkadels or, as I prefer to do, place them on an oiled oven tray and bake them at 200°C for 30 minutes.
- Another option is to make an Italian-Style Tomato Sauce (see page 177).
- Brown the frikkadels in a pan and then place them in the sauce, either on the stove or in the oven until cooked.

Enjoy hot or cold with a nice fresh salad.

TIP: These make ideal burgers or, pressed into a loaf pan, a meat loaf. You would then bake the loaf for an hour at 170°C.

PIAZZA

PASTAS & PESTOS

Fresh Pasta

You can make pasta without a machine if you have a good rolling pin and a strong arm, but a small pasta maker is a handy tool to have. Passing the dough through the rollers will knead it and then cut it for you at the turn of the handle. It requires some practice, but once you get the hang of it, it is great fun to do. Both my boys grew up cranking a pasta maker's handle, especially in the hectic lead-up to the Grahamstown Festival. We would make boxes and boxes of pasta beforehand, as it was impossible to keep up with demand during the festival. Once the pasta has dried, it keeps very well if you keep it sealed and dry. The ingredients below are enough for 6 people.

- 500g flour (I use a whole-wheat or bread flour; if you can source Italian durum wheat, use that)
- 4 free-range eggs

- Put the flour into a mixing bowl, make a hole in the middle and pour the eggs into it.
- Using a fork, mix the eggs into the flour until they have blended completely.
- You will now need to knead with your hands. If the dough is too wet, add more flour; if it's too dry, add a little water.
- Flour the table you are working on, tip the dough onto the table and knead until it becomes elastic.
- Cut the dough into several pieces – you will learn the most suitable size through trial and error.
- I use a rolling pin to roll the first piece flat before starting to use the machine. Keep the other dough covered.
- Now follow your machine's instructions.
- Once the pasta has been cut, I use a clothes horse to dry it on. I have, in the past, used broom-handles and all sorts of other things.
- Good luck – the taste and texture of fresh pasta cannot be compared to the dried variety.

Festival Pasta with Ham and Mushrooms

This was always the most popular sauce at Lynn's Trattoria during the Grahamstown Festival in the '90s. Served with homemade pasta and shaved Parmesan, we could hardly keep up with the demand. My student cooks each had their own version of this sauce and no one bothered to measure anything in the hectic demand, but somehow each sauce had its own delicious flavour.

- 500g linguine pasta (enough for 4–5 adults)
- 400–500g brown or white mushrooms, sliced
- ground black pepper
- 1 tbsp butter
- 1 tbsp (15 ml) olive oil
- 2 cloves garlic, crushed
- 400g of any cooked ham (you can get away with a cheap ham here), sliced thinly
- 100 ml dry white wine
- 400 ml fresh or sour cream
- salt to taste
- chopped parsley and shaved Parmesan to garnish

- Cook the pasta 'al dente'. Add some extra virgin olive oil to the pasta as soon as it has been drained.
- Grind the pepper over the mushrooms and fry in butter and olive oil with the garlic over a high heat.
- As soon as the mushrooms start to shrink, add the ham, wine and cream.
- Keep stirring while the sauce simmers and thickens.
- Taste before adding salt, as the ham is often salty.
- Garnish with parsley and Parmesan, serving immediately.

Beetroot Sauce for Pasta

- 1 beetroot, cooked
- 4 tbsp (60 ml) extra virgin olive oil (use the Tokara Premium as it has an intense flavour, which marries well with the beetroot)
- 2 cloves garlic, crushed
- 2 tsp fresh lemon juice
- ½ tsp sugar (optional)
- ½ tsp salt
- ½ cup fresh parsley, chopped finely

- Blend all of the ingredients, except the parsley, adding more oil if too dry.
- Stir sauce into pasta, or top pasta with sauce.
- Sprinkle with parsley.

Serve with 250g linguine or spaghetti and a variety of fresh salad leaves.

TIP: Sprinkle with 2 tbsp roasted macadamia or pine nuts as an optional extra and freshly grated Parmesan cheese.

Liberty
400ml

Maldon

Fresh Basil, Rocket or Parsley Pesto

This pesto sauce is at its best with spaghetti or other long pasta.

- 2–3 cloves garlic
- 1 tsp salt
- 2 handfuls of fresh herbs
- 4 tsp pine nuts or walnuts, chopped
- 125 ml olive oil (extra virgin such as the Tokara Mission)
- 50 g grated Parmesan

- Crush garlic and salt together,
- Chop herbs finely.
- Add everything except cheese.
- Combine thoroughly.
- If using a blender, pulse all ingredients (except Parmesan) together, but not too fine!
- Add the Parmesan.
- The surface of this pesto sauce may blacken if kept for too long. You can remove the black bits and still enjoy it. Adding a film of olive oil will help to prevent this.

TIP: One of my best pastas ever was also the simplest. We were camping on the island of Giglio off the west coast of Italy, near Livorno. The campsite trattoria served a homemade fettucini, which, once cooked, was tossed into a frying pan with the local olive oil and big bits of crushed garlic and salt. Served with Parmesan shavings, it was unbeatable, due to the quality of the oil. The South African oils are every bit as good as the European oils and are usually very much fresher.

Olive Pesto

This was a good festival sauce and I have very fond memories of my mother de-pipping olives and peeling garlic as she helped me at her last Grahamstown Festival before she succumbed to her cancer.

- 2 cloves garlic, crushed
- 2 cups (240 g) seedless black olives
- 5 anchovy fillets
- ¼ cup (70 ml) fresh parsley, chopped
- 1 tsp drained capers
- ½ cup (125 ml) extra virgin olive oil (Tokara Leccino with its subtle fruit and nut character is ideal)

- Blend everything except the olive oil.
- Add olive oil gradually while blending.
- Refrigerate in a covered container – it will keep for 3 days.

Quick and easy, this delicious pesto sauce is good with spaghetti or linguine pasta.

TIP: You could also add a red chilli for some extra bite and serve with shaved Parmesan cheese.

 | NEXT SPREAD: A rare phenomenon occurs when organic matter coagulates as foam during high seas.

VICTORIA-WES 100
WIRELESS FIRST AID

VEGETABLES & SALADS

Baked Aubergine

This dish transforms the humble brinjal into a rich, creamy delight, which can be a main meal or a vegetable accompaniment to something like a meat roast. My friend Jenny's kitchen garden in Riebeek-Kasteel produces wonderful aubergines. Using really fresh produce does make a difference. I would use one aubergine for 2 people, unless they are very small, when you could use 1 per person.

- 2 onions, diced finely
- olive oil (use a robust oil, such as the Frantoio from Tokara)
- 1 tsp ground paprika
- 4 cloves garlic, crushed and chopped roughly
- 2 tins chopped Italian tomatoes
- 2 tbsp chopped fresh oregano
- salt and ground black pepper to taste
- 2 aubergines, cut through with a sharp knife, making 4 lengthwise slits, leaving the stalk side intact
- good squeeze of ½ lemon
- 1 round of feta cheese or handful of grated hard cheese such as mature cheddar or Parmesan (optional)

- Preheat the oven to 180°C.
- Make a tomato sauce by frying the onions in a generous splash of olive oil.
- Add the paprika and garlic. Add the tomato and cook until thick over a high heat.
- Add the oregano and seasoning and stir well.
- Place aubergines in a baking dish oiled with olive oil.
- Using your hands to hold the aubergine and force the slits open, spoon the tomato sauce in between the slits – it will run over, which is fine.
- Squeeze the lemon over the aubergines and cover with a lid or tin foil.
- Bake for 45 minutes. Remove the lid and bake for a further 15 minutes.
- If this is your main meal, sprinkle with crumbled feta or other cheese before serving.

A variation on this recipe is to slice the aubergines thinly. You do not need to peel them.

Layer the aubergines in a flat oven dish with the tomato sauce and a sprinkling of cheese, ending with sauce and cheese on top. Use more cheese than you would for the recipe.

Bake uncovered for about 35 minutes. By then it should be bubbling and brown.

Melt in the mouth goodness!

Green Beans

When my boys were travelling the world, I would get phone calls to please explain how I cooked my green beans. Jesse, in particular, loved this vegetable done in this simple way. Remember that the quality of the beans will determine the end product.

- fresh green beans, left whole with only the stalk-end removed
- 1–2 garlic cloves, crushed
- extra-virgin olive oil (Tokara's Mission oil with its mild and gentle flavour is good here, as you don't want to overpower the beans)
- salt flakes to taste

- I usually use my waterless steel pots to cook my vegetables in or I steam them in a bamboo steamer. Either way, the beans must not be overdone. I test by breaking a bean with my fingers. If it breaks easily, it's done.
- Place the beans in your serving dish and toss immediately with olive oil, garlic and salt.
- Good hot or at room temperature.

Grilled Mushrooms

Obie loves these and says that they are as good as steak and easier to chew. This is also a good starter for a main meal.

- big brown mushrooms (1 per person as a main meal)
- extra-virgin olive oil (the Tokara Mission, with its light, delicate taste, is ideal)
- 1 sprig fresh oregano per mushroom, finely chopped
- salt and ground black pepper to taste
- 1 garlic clove per mushroom, crushed

- Rub olive oil onto the mushroom cap and place it cap down onto a baking dish.
- Pour some olive oil into the mushroom.
- Sprinkle with oregano, pepper, salt and garlic.
- Grill under a preheated grill for about 10 minutes, depending on the size of your mushrooms.

Enjoy hot or at room temperature with salad or vegetables of your choice.

Roast Beetroot, Butternut and Sweet Potato

These root vegetables can be roasted separately or together. They can be prepared and left to cool for a salad or served straight from the oven to accompany a roast. The beetroot takes a little longer, but is really good with a bit of a crunch, so I do mix mine.

- veggies: as many as desired
- fresh ginger, peeled and sliced (I love ginger, so tend to be generous, and besides, it's good for you!)
- olive oil to coat
- 1–2 oranges, squeezed
- salt to taste
- herbs: sage or rocket (if as a salad)
- nuts: any roasted nuts or pumpkin seeds, sprinkled onto the room temperature vegetables (if as a salad)
- balsamic vinegar (if as a salad)

TIP: Cut your leeks (the firm white parts) into bite-sized pieces, steam them and add to your salad with a generous sprinkling of herbs.

- Preheat the oven to 200°C.
- Peel and chop the vegetables into similar sizes. Pour on some olive oil and use your hands to coat the veggies and ginger.
- Pour over the orange juice, amount depending on the veggies – I also add slivers of orange skin. There should be a shallow layer of juice in the bottom of the oven dish or pan.
- Bake for about 50–60 minutes. Add the sage 15 minutes before removing from the oven, when you give the veggies a stir.

Sprinkle with salt before serving.

This way of roasting makes for a dry roasted vegetable. If you prefer your vegetables softer, cover the roasting pan. If using as a room temperature salad, sprinkle with rocket, nuts and balsamic vinegar when cool.

Baked Spinach or Swiss Chard

This dish is a good starter for a dinner party. We eat it as a main meal with a vegetable such as roast butternut or beetroot.

- 2 medium-sized onions, finely chopped
- 2 cloves of garlic, crushed
- olive oil
- 1 large bunch Swiss chard, stalks removed, steamed, chopped (if using small-leafed spinach, steam and chop)
- 4 eggs
- 150 ml milk, fresh cream (or sour cream)
- pinch of freshly grated nutmeg
- salt and ground black pepper to taste
- 100 g Parmesan or other hard cheese
- 8 small Roma tomatoes (approximately)

- Preheat the oven to 190°C.
- Fry the onion and garlic in a little olive oil.
- Making sure that the spinach has been squeezed dry, stir-fry quickly with the onion and garlic.
- Put into a deep baking dish or divide into 4 small individual oven dishes.
- Beat the eggs and milk or cream together and add the seasoning.
- Pour onto the spinach, letting the egg mixture soak through the spinach.
- Sprinkle with the Parmesan.
- A nice touch is to press some whole little Roma tomatoes into the top so that they remain visible.
- Bake uncovered for 30 minutes or until set – the centre must be firm to the touch.

Sweetcorn Fritters with Sweet Chilli Sauce

The first time I ate these was with my son Nic in a Thai restaurant in Cape Town. When my good friend Jenny had some left-over cooked sweetcorn, she found a recipe for fritters in one of her cookbooks. I have since adapted that recipe and here it is, with a wonderful blend of spices to compliment the sweetcorn. It's a good snack, starter for 4 people, or could be a meal served with a salad for 2–3 people.

FRITTERS

- ½ cup ground rice flour (or bread flour)
- ½ cup bread flour
- ¼ tsp baking powder
- ½ tsp salt
- 1 tsp ground cumin
- 1 tsp ground coriander (or paprika or both)
- ½ cup (125 ml) water or the juice from the sweetcorn tin
- 1 free-range egg, beaten
- 1 tsp lemon juice
- 2 cups (500 ml) sweetcorn kernels (either a tin or kernels from 3 large cooked cobs)
- 4 spring onions, finely sliced (or a small red onion, finely diced)
- ½ red pepper, finely diced
- 3 tbsp fresh coriander or parsley, chopped finely
- olive oil for shallow frying

CHILLI SAUCE

- 3 fresh red chillies, sliced finely
- 1 cup rice vinegar
- 2 tsp salt
- ¾ cup brown sugar
- 1 garlic clove, crushed

FRITTERS

- Add the dry ingredients to the water, egg and lemon juice and whisk until smooth.
- Add the vegetables and herbs and stir well.
- You should be able to make the patties with your floured hands, unless the mixture is too sloppy, in which case, simply add more flour.
- I flour a tray and place the fritters on the tray in preparation for frying. This also allows them to rest, which helps to bind the ingredients together.
- Heat the oil in a pan and shallow-fry until brown, turning once.

CHILLI SAUCE

- Place all the ingredients in a small saucepan.
- Stir until the sugar dissolves and boil for about 10 minutes until the sauce thickens.
- Serve with the fritters.

Frittata Italian Omelette

This is a good way to use leftover vegetables or cooked pasta. You will need a heavy-based pan with an oven-proof handle. An old-fashioned, cast-iron pan works very well. If you don't own one, it is a good investment, as it will last a lifetime.

- olive oil
- 6 free-range eggs, beaten gently with a fork (usually 2 per person)
- salt and ground black pepper to taste
- 1 handful fresh parsley, chopped finely
- any leftover vegetables or a combination of the following: 250g zucchini / baby marrow, cooked, sliced; 250g mushrooms, fried; 100g bacon, fried
- 1 cup (250ml) pasta, cooked
- 6 anchovies (optional)
- 2tbsp Parmesan, grated

- Heat your pan on the stove and preheat the oven's grill, placing the oven rack as high as it can go.
- Cover the bottom of the pan with olive oil.
- Add the eggs and seasoning and cook gently, lifting the sides as they cook with a fork, allowing the uncooked egg to run under the cooked part.
- When the egg looks half done, add the veggies and pasta, pressing it down into the soft top of the omelette.
- If this is a special meal, decorate the top with anchovies.
- Sprinkle the Parmesan over the top and pop under the grill for a few minutes until the cheese has browned and the egg has set.
- This does not take very long and you do not want the egg to be too dry.

Serve with a fresh salad and eat the leftovers cold – equally delicious.

Omelette Strips with a Tomato Sauce

This different Italian dish, using omelette strips instead of pasta, is a real texture–taste sensation. It is also an ideal alternative for those of you doing a low-carb diet. It will make 3 ample portions.

- ¼ cup (60 ml) milk
- 2 tbsp flour
- 10 free-range eggs
- salt and ground black pepper to taste
- 2 tbsp parsley, finely chopped
- olive oil

- Using a whisk, add milk to flour until smooth. Whisk in the eggs and seasoning. Add parsley.
- Using a non-stick pan with olive oil, make thin omelettes, turning once.
- Stack on a wooden board.
- Once finished, cut into strips with a sharp knife.

Serve with a fresh salad.

TIP: Use the recipe for Italian-Style Tomato Sauce (see page 177) – tip the strips into the hot sauce, toss and serve with shaved Parmesan cheese.

Polenta Pie with Spinach and Cheese

This is a wonderful way to eat polenta. You certainly don't think that you are eating maize-meal. It makes a spectacular party dish with its brilliant colours. This quantity will easily feed 6–8 people as an accompaniment to a roast or braai (barbecue).

- 6 cups (1500 ml) water
- salt to taste
- 500 g polenta-type maize-meal (the coarse one if you can get it)
- 200 g hard cheese such as Parmesan, grated (I have used mature cheddar successfully)
- olive oil (or 3 tbsp butter)
- 1 bunch spinach, steamed, chopped
- 1 tin corn kernels, drained
- 1 red pepper, diced
- handful of fresh parsley

- Bring water to boil in a heavy-based pot. Add salt.
- Slowly pour in polenta, stirring until thick. Turn plate onto lowest heat and cover with lid.
- Cook for about 25 minutes – this could vary with all the quick cooking varieties on the market.
- You could follow instructions on your packet, but decrease the amount of water, as you want a really thick porridge.
- Add cheese, oil or butter, spinach, corn, red pepper and parsley. Stir well.
- Transfer to a warmed, oiled serving dish. Press flat and rest for 5 minutes.
- Turn out onto a large serving plate.

Serve with an Italian-Style Tomato Sauce (see page 177) or a Sage Butter (see page 176).

TIP: Leftover polenta will keep well if kept sealed. Wedges can be shallow fried in olive oil or oiled and grilled. Cut into small blocks, it can be added to any salad.

Quiche with Quick Cheese Pastry

The use of the cheese pastry turns this quiche into something special. It is good cold as well as hot. Don't be tempted to use milk instead of cream, as cream gives it a special texture. This quantity will line a large pie dish, which should feed 8 people with a fresh salad.

PASTRY
- 2 cups (500 ml) bread or whole-wheat flour
- 2 cups (500 ml) grated cheddar or other hard cheese
- 250 g butter, cut into blocks (cold)
- pinch of salt
- sprinkling of cayenne pepper

FILLING
- fillings must be cold, and can be virtually anything: stir-fried spinach with garlic and feta cheese, mushrooms, sliced, fried with spinach, any combination of cooked vegetables with or without fried bacon
- whole, raw Roma tomatoes (to cover the pie bottom)
- salt and freshly ground pepper to taste
- 250 ml fresh or sour cream
- 100 ml milk
- 3 extra-large free-range eggs

PASTRY
- Combine all pastry ingredients in your mixer or blender until pastry forms a ball (my Kenwood mixer does this very well).
- Butter a pie dish and press the pastry in evenly with your thumbs.
- Refrigerate or freeze until needed.
- The crust can also be frozen at this stage. I usually double the recipe and make 2, as it is the same amount of work. Then I freeze 1.

FILLING
- Preheat the oven to 230°C.
- Season the filling and spread evenly in pie case over the Roma tomatoes.
- Whisk cream with the milk and the eggs.
- Pour over the filling, letting it seep down to the crust, until just below the rim of the crust.
- Bake for 10 minutes.
- Turn down to 200°C for a further 30 minutes until firm to the touch.

This quiche is also good eaten cold or at room temperature.

 | NEXT SPREAD LEFT: Coastal rocks near the Salt River in Nature's Valley.

Falafel Chickpea Patties

I have good memories of eating my first falafels ever, in the old covered bazaar in Cairo, Khan al Khalili. They were served in warm pita bread with all the trimmings. Back then, in 1994, the boys and I had flown up to meet Obie at the end of his 9-month-long Cape-to-Cairo trip (*Beyond Bagamoyo*). They ran wild in the bazaar as our hotel bordered right onto it. They were always getting lost, but those were happier days and we never felt unsafe. We were woken by the Muezzin's call from the next-door mosque every morning and Obie would run into the street to buy fresh whole-wheat pitas and green onions to eat with our hotel fried eggs. Memories we still taste today. After that trip, Jesse was forever 'tasting Cairo' whenever he ate anything spiced with cumin.

- 500g chickpeas, soaked in water for at least 24 hours (tins are an option)
- 225g onion, chopped
- 2 spring onions, chopped
- 1 bunch fresh parsley (and / or coriander)
- 2–3 cloves garlic
- 1 tsp cayenne pepper
- 1 tsp ground cumin
- 1 tsp sweet paprika
- 25g flour
- salt and ground black pepper to taste
- canola oil

- Blend everything together (except the oil) until quite fine.
- Taste for seasoning and add salt if necessary.
- Flour a board and shape mixture into patties.
- Deep- or shallow-fry in canola oil.

Serve with hummus and a fresh green salad.

TIP: Tzatziki or sweet chilli sauce is also good with falafels. You could also pop a falafel into pita bread, softened rice-paper or a wrap. Add some chopped tomato and any green leaves, top with sauce and enjoy.

 | PREVIOUS SPREAD LEFT: Oil painting by Nigel Mullins.

Ricotta and Spinach Gnocchi

Every good Italian cook has his or her own favourite gnocchi recipe. I started making this recipe years ago and don't even have to stick so closely to the measurements for it to be a success. Your mix must just not be too sloppy, as the gnocchi will then fall apart as it cooks. This will serve 4–6 people.

- 500g fresh spinach, steamed, squeezed very dry and diced really finely
- 50g butter
- 200g ricotta cheese
- 90g white flour (or any other flour)
- 3 free-range egg yolks
- 150g grated Parmesan
- 2ml grated nutmeg
- salt and ground black pepper to taste

- Fry the spinach briefly in the butter to ensure that it is dry. Leave to cool.
- In a bowl, sieve the flour over the ricotta and mix it in gently with a fork.
- Add everything else (including the spinach).
- Check the seasoning.
- Using a very well-floured surface, roll the dough into long thin rolls.
- Cut off even-sized pieces and leave to rest for 30 minutes.
- Meanwhile, bring a large pot of water to the boil.
- Add the gnocchi, one at a time. As they cook, they will float to the surface.
- Keep a warm, oiled serving dish next to the pot and, using a slotted spoon, place the floating gnocchi, one by one, into the dish.

Serve immediately with an Italian-Style Tomato Sauce (see page 177) or a Sage Butter (see page 176).

Rice-Paper Parcels

This was a recipe born of necessity. I didn't have pita breads or the time to make them, so I used rice paper instead.

- sheets of rice paper (if you have the large, plate-sized ones, I would say 3 per person)
- 1½ falafels per person
- hummus
- tzatziki

- Soften the rice paper in warm water, one at a time, as you make the parcels.
- Lay the round of softened rice paper out on a plate. Break each falafel in half.
- Place the piece of falafel on the top half, in the middle.
- Smear a generous amount of hummus on the falafel. Top with some tzatziki.
- Fold the bottom half of the rice paper up, over the filling. Wrap the sides around to make a parcel with the falafel just peeping out of the top.
- Besides looking very decorative, these little parcels are delicious. Eat hot or cold, but they don't keep, as the rice paper tends to go hard.

Good served with a tomato salad.

Asian-Style Stir-Fry

The quantities for this dish will vary according to what vegetables you use. This recipe is merely a guide and is what I usually make for Obie and myself. The preparation is what takes the time – the cooking will not take longer than 10–15 minutes.

- 2 leeks, sliced with the green (or 2 onions, sliced)
- 1 red pepper (or 1 carrot), cut into strips
- 1 handful of glass noodle strands
- 1 handful of dried seaweed
- oil for frying: peanut, sesame or olive oil are all successful
- 3 cloves garlic, crushed
- 1 red chilli (optional)
- ½ a thumb-sized piece of ginger, peeled and sliced thinly
- 12 peas (mange tout or sugar snap)
- 8 mushrooms (or more if you can get the exotic kind)
- 30 ml (2 tbsp) soya sauce to taste
- 15 ml (1 tbsp) oyster sauce
- 15 ml (1 tbsp) fish sauce
- 250 ml coconut milk

- Prepare your vegetables, keeping them separate.
- Soak the noodles in boiling water until just soft. Plunge into cold water.
- Soak the dried seaweed in cold water until it is soft.
- Using a wok or a large frying pan, start frying the leeks / onions in oil
- Add the red pepper / carrot.
- Add garlic, chilli and ginger.
- Add peas and then mushrooms.
- The trick is to add the vegetable needing a longer cooking time first.
- Add the sauces and coconut milk with the seaweed and noodles drained from the cold water.
- Heat through, allowing the flavours to mingle – the veg should be crunchy.

Enjoy the fun way with chopsticks.

Greek Cheese and Spinach Filo Triangles

Obie and I once spent 5 days on the harbour of Alexandropoulos, sleeping in the campsite next to the harbour. We were waiting for the weather to calm down so that we could get to the island of Samothraki. There was only 1 ferry a week. An old Greek man would stroll down to the harbour every morning with a tray of these little pastries, baked by his wife. By the time the weather had calmed down, we were totally addicted.

- 125 ml spring or red onion, chopped
- olive oil
- 500 g steamed spinach, chopped finely
- 60 g feta cheese, crumbled
- 125 ml smooth cottage cheese
- 1 tbsp parsley, chopped
- 2 free-range eggs, lightly beaten
- a good pinch of nutmeg
- salt and ground black pepper to taste
- 125 g filo pastry

TIP: Leftover filling can be baked in a bowl as a crustless quiche.

- Preheat the oven to 180°C.
- Fry the onion in olive oil until soft.
- Add spinach and fry quickly until all moisture has evaporated.
- Place in a mixing bowl and stir in all other ingredients (except filo pastry).
- Cut each sheet of filo pastry into 3 strips.
- Working with one sheet at a time, oil a strip with a pastry brush, and place 1 teaspoon of filling on one end.
- Fold corner of pastry over the filling to form a triangle and continue folding into triangles until the end of the strip.
- Place seam side down on an oiled baking tray. Continue until filling has been used up or you run out of pastry.
- Bake for about 20 minutes until puffed and golden.

LVER WILLOW RD -WEG
BETHESDAWEG STASIE BETHESDA ROAD STATION
Clemensstraße
SANI POLICE POST WIRELESS FIRST AID
BRANDBOONTJIES RIVER
VICTORIA-WES 100

Mediterranean Cauliflower Salad

- 1 cauliflower, steamed
- 8 anchovy fillets
- 2 tbsp capers
- fresh parsley, chopped
- 12 black olives, stoned

DRESSING

- 90 ml (6 tbsp) extra-virgin olive oil (Tokara Frantoio with its intense olive flavour is perfect for this salad)
- 30 ml (2 tbsp) balsamic vinegar (white)
- salt and ground black pepper to taste

- Steam the cauliflower, about 7 minutes for firm florets. Break into small pieces when cool.
- Mix the dressing ingredients together and pour onto the cauliflower and toss well.
- If done while the cauliflower is still warm, more dressing will be absorbed.
- Garnish with the anchovy, capers, parsley and olives.

Roast Butternut Salad

This is a good way to use leftover butternut. There are many possible variations, of which this is only one.

- 1 butternut, diced and coated liberally with extra-virgin olive oil
- pumpkin seeds (optional)
- fresh rocket leaves
- feta cheese or a crumbly goat's milk cheese
- white balsamic vinegar

- Preheat the oven to 200°C.
- Roast the butternut in a shallow oven pan until it starts to brown – this could take up to an hour, depending on your oven and the size of your butternut pieces.
- I often add a sprinkling of pumpkin seeds 10 minutes before I take the butternut out.
- Leave it to cool in the pan.
- Cover a shallow salad bowl with fresh rocket leaves.
- Place the cooled butternut on the leaves and sprinkle with the cheese.
- Finally sprinkle with balsamic vinegar and enjoy.

Broccoli Salad

SALAD

- 1 head of broccoli
- 1 avocado pear
- roasted Macadamia nuts or walnuts, to sprinkle
- 1 small red pepper, sliced as thinly as possible

DRESSING

- 200 ml mild olive oil (I have used the Tokara Mission here as it is mild and gentle)
- 40 ml balsamic vinegar (or fresh lemon juice)
- 1 clove garlic, crushed
- 1 heaped tsp hot mustard
- ½ tsp salt

SALAD

- Steam broccoli until the stalks are just tender and allow to cool.
- Separate the florets and slice the stalks finely.
- Chop the avocado into smallish cubes.
- Chop the nuts coarsely.
- Throw all the ingredients together and dress a good 5 minutes before eating.

DRESSING

- Whisk the garlic, mustard and salt with a little oil to start with and keep adding the rest of the oil.
- Keep whisking as you add the vinegar or lemon juice and the sauce will amalgamate.
- This will make a good cupful of dressing that keeps very well, so only use as much as is needed.

Bean Salad

This salad is not worth making in small quantities, unless you are using tins. I prefer to use dry beans. You can play around with these quantities, depending on your personal taste. The salad keeps well, covered and refrigerated. The dressing is my basic vinaigrette which I use with most fresh salads.

SALAD

- 1 cup (250 ml) cooked red kidney beans
- 1 cup (250 ml) cooked haricot or black-eyed beans
- ½ cup (125 ml) raw mung beans
- 1 cup (250 ml) green beans, steamed whole and cut into bite-size pieces
- 1 bunch spring onions, chopped
- 2 garlic cloves, crushed
- 1 bunch garlic chives or other chives, chopped
- mixed fresh herbs to taste: marjoram, oregano, parsley

DRESSING

- 1 heaped tsp hot English mustard
- 125 ml olive oil, extra virgin, such as the Tokara Leccino
- white balsamic vinegar
- salt and ground black pepper to taste

- Whisk the mustard with olive oil.
- Slowly add about 30 ml vinegar. Whisk and adjust to taste.
- Season with freshly ground black pepper and sea-salt flakes.
- Mix all beans, onions, garlic, chives, herbs and dressing.
- Allow an hour for flavours to be absorbed by the beans.

Red Cabbage Salad

This is a very satisfying, crunchy salad, which will feed 2 people as a side salad.

SALAD

- 1 baby red cabbage (or ¼ large red cabbage), chopped or grated finely
- 4 spring onions, diced
- 1 small bunch garlic chives or other chives, sliced
- 8 walnut halves, broken up
- 1 clove garlic, crushed
- 1 knob of fresh ginger, sliced very thinly (optional, but does give the salad a zing)

DRESSING

- 2 tsp peanut butter (crunchy or smooth)
- 2 tsp runny honey
- 100 ml olive oil (a strong tasting extra virgin is good – Tokara has a premium oil, a fusion of 4 olive variants with pleasant pepper tones)
- balsamic vinegar, a dash or more
- salt to taste

DRESSING

- Make the dressing in a salad bowl.
- Using a whisk, mix the peanut butter and honey.
- Slowly add olive oil until you have a thickish sauce.
- Add vinegar and salt to taste.
- Add salad ingredients to the dressing half an hour before serving.

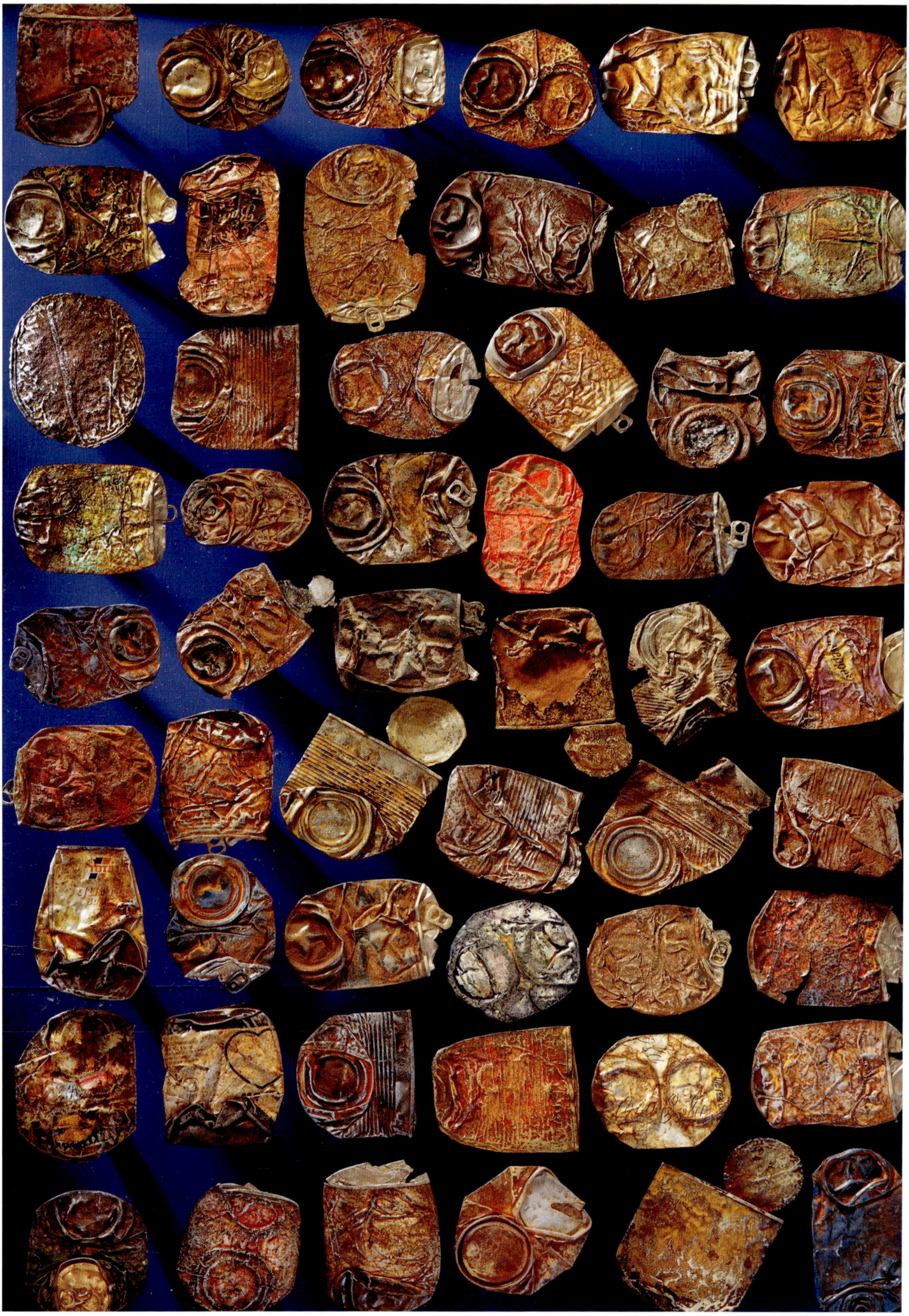

Kodak
'KODET' LENS
Brownie Flash II
CAMERA
MADE IN ENGLAND BY KODAK LIMITED LONDON
KODAK REFLEX
67 II
KODET LENS
Kodak
DUAFLEX CAMERA
MADE IN TORONTO
Corona
Rapide
ENGLAND
MENISCUS
FLASH METER V
ISO
MINOLTA
WINDAR LENS
Nikon
NIKKOR-P·C Auto 1:2.5 f=105mm
SMC PENTAX
8610754
Super-Multi
JAPAN

DIPS, SPREADS & SAUCES

Chicken Liver Paté the Italian Way

This recipe is adapted from one of my Italian cookery courses. The sweet wine adds something special and I prefer it to the creamier patés.

- 1 x 250-g punnet chicken livers
- 6 fresh sage leaves
- 2 cloves garlic, crushed
- ground black pepper
- 30 ml olive oil
- ½ cup good sweet red wine
- salt to taste
- 1 anchovy fillet
- 1 tbsp capers
- 1 free-range egg yolk
- little milk

- Fry the livers, sage, garlic and black pepper in olive oil for about 10 minutes, until the liver has lost its red colour. Stir constantly.
- Add the wine and salt and cook to reduce the wine a bit.
- Add the anchovy, capers and egg yolk.
- Blend the paté – add a little milk if too thick.
- Check seasoning.

TIP: This paté is delicious with toast. Take slices of French bread or ciabatta, brush both sides with olive oil and grill both sides until brown. Use extra-virgin oil, something like a Tokara Frantoio, which has an intense olive flavour. For those of you not eating bread, it makes a good dip for celery sticks or cucumber.

Tzatziki

This yoghurt and cucumber sauce is a delicious condiment.

- 1 long cucumber, grated and squeezed dry
- 1 garlic clove, crushed with a little salt
- 500 ml plain Greek yoghurt
- 2 tsp extra-virgin olive oil
- 2 tsp lemon juice
- 1 tsp fresh mint, dill, coriander or parsley, finely chopped

- Mix all ingredients together well.
- Keep cold until using.

TIP: Excellent inside a falafel pita (use mint or parsley), with a hot curry (use coriander) or with fish (use dill).

Hummus Bi Tahini

This thick, creamy paste is delicious on fresh, crusty bread or as an accompaniment to Falafel Chickpea Patties (see page 142) or Sweetcorn Fritters (see page 126). It keeps a good week in the fridge.

- 175g chickpeas
- 2 cloves garlic, crushed
- 2 lemons, squeezed
- 150ml tahini paste (ground sesame seeds) or peanut butter
- 1tbsp olive oil (I enjoy the fullness of the Frantoio oil for hummus)
- 2tbsp parsley, finely chopped
- salt and ground black pepper to taste

- For the chickpea purée you could use a tin or make it from scratch (there is a difference in taste).
- To make: soak the chickpeas overnight and then cook for about 2 hours, until soft. Add salt.
- Drain and keep some of the cooking water.
- Blend until smooth, adding as much of the water as necessary to get the sauce smooth.
- Then add all of the rest of the ingredients to the purée.
- Taste before seasoning.

Sage Butter

This must be one of the easiest, quickest sauces ever. It is delicious with pasta or polenta.

- a good handful of fresh sage leaves, chopped
- 200g butter

- Melt butter in frying pan.
- Add sage when butter is nice and hot.
- Fry until crispy – careful now as the butter will turn brown, but you do not want the sage to burn.
- Use immediately.

Italian-Style Tomato Sauce

- 1 smallish onion, finely chopped
- olive oil for frying
- ½ a small carrot, finely chopped
- 1 stalk celery, with the leaves, finely chopped
- 2 cloves garlic, crushed
- a handful of fresh sweet basil or parsley, finely chopped
- 1 tsp sweet paprika
- 1 chilli (optional)
- 4 anchovy fillets (optional)
- 2 tins whole or chopped Italian tomatoes (I prefer tins to fresh, unless you have really ripe fresh tomatoes)
- salt and ground black pepper to taste

- Fry onion in olive oil for a few minutes.
- Add carrot, celery, garlic, herbs and spices. Stir-fry gently until veg is softish.
- Add tomatoes and simmer, crushing any big lumps of tomato.
- Simmer until sauce becomes thick.
- Check seasoning.

TIP: This sauce is worth making in large quantities as it freezes well and will keep in the fridge for about 3 days. Anchovy fillets are a good addition – add with the veg but take care when adding the salt. When I did my Italian cookery course with Lorenza de Medici, she said that she always added anchovy to her tomato sauce. Interestingly enough, you don't even taste the anchovy, but it does add richness to the sauce.

MOLLY'S

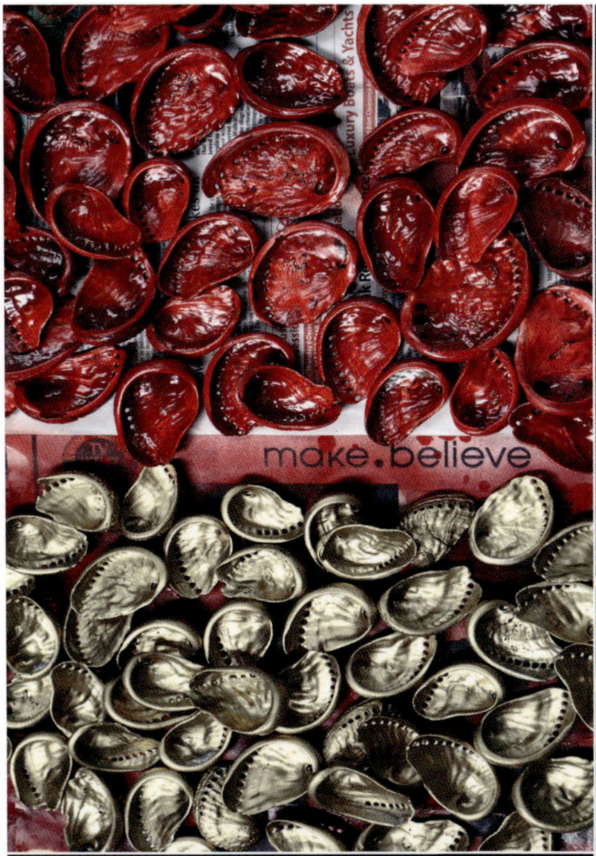
make.believe

MOST
BEAUTIFUL
LAMPSHADE
IN THE
WORLD

Almond Tart

This was originally my friend Linny Badenhorst's recipe. We both love marzipan!

- 125 g soft butter
- ¾ cup (180 ml) castor sugar
- 2 cups (500 ml) cake flour
- 1 tsp baking powder
- 2 free-range eggs, beaten
- 1 x 250-g pkt marzipan
- whole almonds (optional)

- Preheat the oven to 180°C.
- Cream butter and sugar well.
- Add all other ingredients and knead well.
- Press into 2 small or 1 large shallow buttered cake tin.
- An option here is to press whole almonds into the dough, making a pattern around the edge.
- Smooth the top with a little milk and bake for 30 minutes.
- Cool in tin before removing.

Apple Crumble Pie

What makes this pie different is the freshly grated apple and the easy 'press-in' pastry.

- 125g soft butter
- ½ cup (125ml) brown sugar
- 1 beaten free-range egg
- 2 cups (500ml) bread or whole-wheat flour
- 2 level tsp baking powder
- 1 tsp ground cinnamon
- walnuts and sesame seeds (optional)
- 5–6 apples (Granny Smith work really well)
- 3 cloves and some raisins (optional)

- Cream the butter and sugar well.
- Add the egg and then the dry ingredients. Mix well.
- Divide pastry in half. Press half into a buttered pie dish and refrigerate the other half for at least 30 minutes. This can be done 1–2 days before you make your pie.
- You can also freeze the piecrust and the other pastry at this stage.
- Preheat the oven to 180–200°C.
- Peel, core and grate the apples.
- Flatten the grated apple into the prepared pastry in the pie dish. Add cloves and raisins if desired.
- Grate the other half of the dough over the apple and sprinkle with walnuts or sesame seeds if you want some added healthy crunch.
- Bake for 30 minutes.

Serve with fresh cream, custard or thick, creamy Greek yoghurt.

Baked Cheesecake

This is a recipe that I used during my catering days. Jesse loved cheesecake, so the search was always on for the perfect cheesecake. This is mine! The delicious baked cake has no crust. You will need a well-buttered, loose-bottomed 260-mm cake tin.

- 500g cream cheese
- 500g smooth cottage cheese
- 300g white sugar
- 4 extra-large free-range eggs
- 30g (50ml) cake flour
- 25g (50ml) cornflour
- 125g melted butter, cooled
- 1tsp vanilla essence and / or 2tsp lemon zest
- 2 cups (500ml) sour cream
- 1 cup (250ml) fresh cream

TIP: Sprinkled with fresh berries, this makes a really decorative cake. You could also heat a berry jam with extra fresh berries added, then cool and spoon onto your cheesecake. This is especially handy when the cake cracks slightly when baking.

- Preheat the oven to 165°C.
- Cream both cheeses very well, using an electric mixer, for about 10 minutes. Add sugar slowly while beating and continue for 5 more minutes.
- Beat eggs with a whisk and add to mixture. Beat well.
- Sift flour and cornflour and beat into mixture with melted butter, vanilla and lemon zest. Beat for 5 minutes.
- Stir in the 2 creams until well blended.
- Pour mixture into a buttered tin and bake for 1 hour.
- The cake should be light brown and appear firm.
- Switch oven off and leave cake inside to cool for at least 3 hours.
- Refrigerate for a good 2 hours before removing the sides of the cake tin.
- Cheesecake will keep for at least 5 days in the fridge.

AMSTEL

Jack Wolfskin

Chocolate Mousse

This is a fairly traditional mousse. It is easy to make and has a good texture. My good friend Micky gave me this recipe a very long time ago, when this was the ultimate desert. I still make it every now and then, to much acclaim.

- 200g good quality dark chocolate (about 80%)
- 3tbsp espresso coffee, coffee liquor or brandy
- 1tbsp butter
- 3 free-range eggs, separated

- Melt chocolate with coffee in the top of a double boiler – use a heat-resistant bowl in a pot of water!
- Stir in butter. Remove from heat.
- Add egg yolks, folding in well.
- Fold in whisked whites very well.
- Pour mousse into individual bowls or glasses.
- Refrigerate for at least 2 hours before serving.

Serve with a blob of thick, fresh cream and / or chocolate shavings.

 I PREVIOUS SPREAD: Terns and sunset over the Grootrivier lagoon.

Lindt
Lindt

Panna Cotta Italian-Style

This is my friend Linny's favourite dessert, which I have adapted. It makes 4 generous servings.

- 2 vanilla pods (or some form of vanilla essence)
- 2 cups (500 ml) coconut milk (or ½ coconut, ½ full-cream milk)
- 2 cups (500 ml) thick fresh cream
- 100 g white sugar
- 2 leaves gelatine (or the appropriate amount of granular gelatine for 1 litre of liquid)

TIP: Linny serves her Panna Cotta with a drizzle of fresh puréed berries.

- If using vanilla pods, split them and scrape out the seeds. You can simply use the whole pod, which you remove before adding the gelatine.
- Add the seeds to the coconut milk and fresh cream in a deepish saucepan.
- Add the sugar and bring to the boil, stirring now and again.
- Soak the gelatine leaves in a little water until they have partially dissolved. Add the leaves to the cream mix when it starts to boil.
- Simmer gently for a minute or 2. Remove from the heat and decant into a large bowl.
- Place the bowl over another bowl filled with ice and stir gently.
- The mix should start to set after about ½ an hour. Whisk well and pour mix into individual serving bowls or one large serving bowl.
- Refrigerate for at least 2 hours before serving – you could make this dessert the day before needed.

Pavlova

This is a colourful, melt-in-the-mouth, festive dessert. It has become my favourite Christmas pudding as colourful berries are in season and most of the work can be done a couple of days before Christmas. You need a strong arm and a whisk to make the meringue without an electric beater, but it is possible. This will easily satisfy 4–6 people.

MERINGUE

- 5 free-range egg whites
- 290g castor sugar
- 1 tsp vanilla essence
- 2 tsp cornflour
- white vinegar

CUSTARD

- 125g white sugar
- 5 free-range egg yolks
- 40g flour
- 2 cups (500 ml) milk
- 1 vanilla pod or 1 tsp vanilla essence

TIP: To serve, you can top it with custard, sprinkle with berries or chopped soft fruit and decorate with fresh cream. If you're not using custard, you could pile the meringue high with whipped cream and sprinkle it with berries.

MERINGUE

- Preheat the oven to 140°C.
- Beat egg whites until they form peaks. Slowly add the sugar and vanilla essence, beating continuously.
- Mix cornflour with the vinegar until it is a pourable, solid-looking liquid.
- Add this to the meringue and continue beating – it should have a smooth, shiny look to it.
- 'Spray and Cook' 2 average-sized pie plates or any large, flattish, ovenproof dish.
- Using a spatula, spread the meringue in a swirling motion, making the sides slightly higher than the bottom.
- You can use a big decorative plate that can be used in the oven or cover a baking tray with tin foil – I prefer using the dish I am going to serve the Pavlova in, as it can be difficult to move it without breaking it.
- Bake for 1 hour, turn the heat off and leave to cool in the oven to prevent cracking.
- The Pavlova base can be made a few days in advance as long as it is kept moisture free in a tin or plastic bag. Use a clean refuse bag if you are using a really big dish.

CUSTARD

- Whisk the sugar and egg yolks until thick.
- Gradually work in the flour.
- Heat the milk and vanilla until boiling point.
- Gradually whisk in the egg mix and bring to the boil, stirring continuously. Remove the pod if using.
- Allow to cool, covering the top with a sheet of plastic to prevent a skin forming.
- This custard will keep for at least 2 days in the fridge.

Rice Pudding

I first tasted this Middle-Eastern type of rice pudding in Istanbul in 1970. You need time (a good hour) to make this pudding, but it's certainly worth it.

- 1 cup (250 ml) water
- 4 tbsp short-grained rice (Arborio works well)
- 1 litre milk
- 2 tbsp cornflour
- ½ cup (125 ml) sugar
- 1 tsp vanilla essence (or 1 pod) and / or 1 tsp grated lemon rind
- cinnamon

- Boil water, add rice and simmer for 15 minutes.
- Add milk (and vanilla pod if using) and simmer for 30 minutes, stirring occasionally.
- Mix cornflour with 4 tbsp water. Add to rice mix slowly and keep stirring.
- Add sugar and simmer for 15 minutes.
- Remove from heat, add vanilla essence and lemon rind and pour into 1 large or 4 small individual bowls.
- Sprinkle with cinnamon and enjoy at room temperature or chilled.

Fruit and Nut Cake

This is a cake to dream of – no flour, no butter, no sugar.

- 3 extra-large free-range eggs
- 2 tbsp (30 ml) runny honey
- 1 tsp vanilla or almond essence
- 75 ml brandy
- 250 g each of chopped dates and mixed dried fruit
- 250 g red, green, yellow glacé cherries (any combination or only one colour)
- 350 g mixed nuts: walnuts, pecans, almonds (once again, any combination is good)
- 1 tsp each of cinnamon and mixed spice
- 100 g ground almonds
- ½ tsp baking powder
- extra brandy to pour on after baking

- Preheat the oven to 150°C.
- Beat the eggs with an electric beater until thick.
- Add the honey, essence and brandy.
- Combine the fruit, nuts, spice and baking powder and mix together with the eggs.
- Spread evenly into 2 loose-bottomed cake tins, lined with foil and greased.
- Bake for an hour.
- Pour a little brandy over the hot cakes.
- Cool in tins. Slow your cooling time down by covering the cake in its tin with a blanket.
- Wrapped in tin foil, this cake will keep for a month.

 I OPPOSITE: Moonrise over Nature's Valley beach. I NEXT SPREAD: The Nature's Valley lagoon.

Jenny's Rich, Dark Chocolate Cake

This cake was a firm favourite during my catering and festival years. I once traded 3 cakes for a handmade cotton jersey. The jersey outlasted the cakes!

- 3 cups (750 ml) cake flour
- 1 cup (250 ml) cocoa
- 15 ml baking powder
- 3 cups (750 ml) white sugar
- a pinch of salt
- 250 g melted butter
- 15 ml vanilla essence
- 1½ cups (375 ml) milk
- 3 extra-large free-range eggs
- ¼ cup fresh cream

- Preheat the oven to 160°C.
- Sift flour, cocoa and baking powder. Add the rest of the dry ingredients.
- Add the butter, vanilla essence and milk.
- Add the eggs one by one while beating.
- Add the cream. Stir well.
- Using 2 well-buttered or sprayed cake tins, pour cake mix in and bake in a slow oven for about 1 hour, until baked through. Remove from tins and cool on a wire rack.

TIP: Decorate with butter icing, caramel, fresh whipped cream or a chocolate glaze. My favourite is to use tinned caramel in between the 2 layers and then a dark melted chocolate thinned with fresh cream to an easy pouring consistency as a glaze.

 PREVIOUS SPREAD: The Grootrivier beyond the bridge.

Aunty Isabel's Traditional Christmas Cake

I used to make this cake by hand before I invested in a big Kenwood mixer, so it is possible, just much lighter work with an electric beater. My aunt Issy (she hated being called Issy, although as kids we just ignored this) was one of my mom's sisters. She married a German farmer from the Wartburg district in KwaZulu-Natal, a truly gentle, lovely man. She was a nursing sister / matron of note, more German than Onkel Herbert. My brother David and I spent many very happy holidays on the farm with our 3 cousins, Nola, Glenda and Carmen; often joined by others from the Du Plessis clan. Aunt Issy's kitchen was an experience of culinary aromatherapy. She baked huge farm breads for us hungry kids, which we devoured with farm butter and homemade jams.

- 500g each of sultanas, raisins and currants
- 250g fruit peel
- 250g glacé cherries
- 170ml brandy
- 500g soft butter
- 500g brown sugar
- 10 extra-large free-range eggs, separated
- 500g cake or bread flour
- ½tsp each of ground cloves and nutmeg
- 2tsp each of cinnamon and mixed spice
- ½tsp salt
- 1tsp bicarbonate of soda
- 500g each of almonds or walnuts
- extra brandy to pour on after baking

- Preheat the oven to 130°C.
- Mix all fruit and soak in brandy overnight.
- Cream butter and sugar well.
- Add egg yolks and mix. Keep mixing as you add flour, spices, salt and bicarb.
- Add fruit and nuts. Mix well.
- Beat egg whites to a thick foam.
- Using your hands, add egg whites, mixing really well.
- Grease and line a square cake tin (250ml) with greaseproof paper or tin foil – do a double layer on the bottom.
- Bake in a slow oven for 4 hours. You might have to cover the top of the cake with a piece of foil for the last hour if it looks like it's burning.
- Remove from oven and pour over some extra brandy.
- Wrap cake (in tin) for a good while so that it cools down really slowly – I wrap it in a towel and then a duvet. You can leave it overnight.
- Remove from tin and wrap in tin foil. This cake will keep for months if you splash it with some brandy every now and then.

TIP: You can either marzipan and ice the cake or just decorate with nuts on the top, stuck on with a layer of honey heated with brandy.

Carrot Cake

This is a very old recipe, which was used extensively during my Grahamstown Festival days. It has the advantage of being quick and easy with no fancy ingredients.

- 1 cup (250 ml) brown sugar
- 1 cup (250 ml) canola oil or 1 cup (250 ml) melted butter
- 3 extra-large free-range eggs
- 1 cup (250 ml) bread flour
- 1 cup (250 ml) whole-wheat flour
- 10 ml baking powder
- 1 tsp cinnamon
- ½ tsp mixed spice
- 2 cups (500 ml) grated carrots
- 100 g coarsely chopped walnuts or pecan nuts (optional)
- ½ cup sultanas (optional)

ICING

- 250 g icing sugar
- lemon juice

- Preheat the oven to 180°C.
- Beat sugar and oil (or butter) well.
- Add eggs, beating well.
- Add all dry ingredients with carrots, nuts and sultanas.
- Mix well and pour into a well-greased or sprayed cake tin (I like using a tin with a hole in the middle).
- Bake for about 40 minutes.
- Turn out onto a rack to cool.

ICING

- Ice with an easy lemon glaze.
- Whisk icing sugar with enough lemon juice to make a thick, pouring consistency.
- Pour onto the cooled cake.
- You could also fold some rich cream cheese into this glaze.

Greek Butter Cookies

These are shortbread-like cookies that are delicious served with tea or coffee.

- 200 g unsalted soft butter (I often use salted butter)
- 1 cup (250 ml) castor sugar
- 1 free-range egg yolk
- 1 tbsp brandy
- approximately 3 cups (750 ml) cake flour
- ½ tsp baking powder
- cloves
- 500 g icing sugar

- Preheat the oven to 170°C.
- Cream butter and castor sugar very well. Stir in egg yolk and brandy.
- Add flour with baking powder, a little at a time, until you have a soft dough that you can knead until smooth – I do all of this in my Kenwood mixer.
- Shape small pieces of dough into golf-ball-sized pieces.
- Insert a clove into the top of each and place on a buttered or sprayed baking sheet.
- Bake for about 20 minutes.
- While they are still warm, sift icing sugar over them to coat well.

Oat Crunchies

My friend Linny gave me this recipe many moons ago, when I was looking for healthy snacks for my boys. When I was training English Channel swimmers while teaching at the DSG in Grahamstown, the girls would wolf these crunchies down after an hour's freezing swim in the Settlers Dam or the Cowie River.

- 500 g butter
- 2 tbsp syrup
- 2 tsp bicarbonate of soda
- 2 cups (500 ml) bread flour
- 4 cups (1 litre) oats
- 1 cup (250 ml) raisins
- 2 cups (500 ml) desiccated coconut
- 2 cups (500 ml) brown sugar

- Preheat the oven to 120 °C.
- Melt butter with syrup.
- Add bicarb and stir until frothy.
- Add the rest of the ingredients and mix well.
- Bake for 45 minutes.
- Cut in tin while warm.
- Cool in tin and store in an airtight container.

FREE COUNTRY
DEON MEYER
DEON MEYER
en ander verhale
DEON MEYER
INFANTA

Date Balls

My friend Rachel managed to get this recipe, which I have adapted slightly, from one of her Hindu friends. They are a really healthy snack or addition to a cheese board. This amount will make about 30 golf-ball-sized balls.

- 500g dried dates, pitted
- 200ml water
- 1½ cups raw oats
- 1 cup (250ml) desiccated coconut
- 80ml sesame or poppy seeds
- 80ml toasted sunflower or chopped pumpkin seeds
- 75g chopped almonds, hazelnuts, pecans or walnuts
- extra coconut for coating

- Bring dates to the boil in the water, turn the heat off, put a lid on the pot and let it stand for 30 minutes.
- Blend the dates to a purée or use a potato masher.
- Mix in the rest of the ingredients – if too soggy, add more oats.
- Using the extra coconut in your hands, shape the mixture into balls to the size of your choice.
- Stored in a sealed container in the fridge, they will keep for at least a week.

 | NEXT SPREAD LEFT: Sea moss on the rocks at Sinker Bay. RIGHT: Organic foam patterns.

INDEX

 I PREVIOUS SPREAD: The Grootrivier estuary mouth at Nature's Valley.

When Tokara first started pressing their olives, I happened to be there for a first pressing. I took a bottle filled with the incredibly aromatic oil to my kitchen. This was my introduction to what is now South Africa's bounty of olive oils. My friend, Micky Ferreira, realised a dream with her olives and the resultant Tokara delicatessen. In turn, she has enabled me to realise a dream – one you are holding in your hands.

TOKARA
STELLENBOSCH

First published by Jacana Media (Pty) Ltd
in 2014

10 Orange Street
Sunnyside
Auckland Park 2092
South Africa
+2711 628 3200
www.jacana.co.za

ISBN: 978-1-4314-1068-2

Design and layout by MR Design
Set in Trade Gothic
Printed by Craft Print International Ltd
Job no. 002219

See a complete list of Jacana titles at
www.jacana.co.za

Thank you Marius Roux, for being excited enough by Obie's images to make a 'mock-up' of the book that inspired Bridget Impey of Jacana Media to believe in our project.

All images in the book were taken at Nature's Valley.